Wor Jackie
THE JACKIE MILBURN STORY

WOR JACKIE

The
JACKIE MILBURN
Story

by
John Gibson

SPORTSPRINT PUBLISHING
EDINBURGH

Dedication

To Laura Milburn with love and affection
and to Jackie Junior, Betty and Linda.

John Donald Publishers Ltd.,
138 St. Stephen Street, Edinburgh EH3 5AA.

ISBN 0 85976 297 1

Phototypeset by Beecee Typesetting Services
Printed and bound in Great Britain by Billings & Sons Ltd., Worcester

Acknowledgements

My grateful thanks to Laura Milburn for giving the whole idea her blessing. I wouldn't have worked on the book without it. Thanks, too, to daughter Betty and to brother-in-law Les Common for invaluable help and to Jackie's sister Mavis for the countless cups of tea and biscuits. For Jackie's record as a professional runner I owe a debt to Ossie Oswald, who provided so much detail from his vast records and marvellous memory.

Producing a book requires a good team round you, and my appreciation goes to John Tuckwell and Donald Morrison of John Donald Publishers for their enthusiasm on the venture, to Mona Southern for help with reading the transcript, and to Tracie Southern for ferrying me all over the North East and providing moral support.

Photographs are produced courtesy of the *Newcastle Chronicle and Journal Ltd*, the *Belfast Evening Telegraph* and from Jackie's personal family album.

Contents

Introduction

Wor Jackie was a lot of things to a lot of people . . . a master craftsman, a source of hope, an entertainer, a gentleman, a man with the common touch.

He was also Roy of the Rovers, a swashbuckling centre-forward in the days of brylcreemed hair and baggy shorts when soccer grounds were full to bursting and his magical goals were the lifeblood of Newcastle United. He was an ordinary pit lad from Ashington who made dreams come true yet never strayed from his roots. A man with a simple charm.

To me he was both a hero and a firm friend. I grew from boyhood adulation to genuine friendship. A helping hand was always there. And I've always believed that Jackie helped me gain the ultimate recognition in my profession — when I was voted Provincial Sportswriter of the Year in 1981, the first award of its kind ever given, two of my six submitted articles were on Jackie Milburn.

If I've written his fascinating lifestory with love and warmth then I offer no apology. It couldn't have been written any other way if you knew the man. But it is also a true story, a life which touched the hearts of millions.

The streets were lined with 30,000 tearful folk at his funeral more than 30 years after he last wore the black and white shirt of Newcastle. He was so loved United named their new stand after him. An award-winning musical was written in his honour, and a bronze statue of Wor Jackie in action was commissioned to stand in the city centre. All for a man who, as Jackie once said, 'only kicked a footbaal.'

But, my, didn't he do it well!

John Gibson

CHAPTER ONE

The Beginning

Cobbled streets with back to back houses and outside netties, pit heaps dominating the skyline and miners, dirty and dusty, walking in knee pads with tin helmets and their bait on their backs. That was Ashington, a mining town in Northumberland, just after the First World War. A typical northern community of good humoured working folk with not a lot of money to spend on life's little luxuries but not complainers about life's drudgery.

Within the town, as within the bowels of the earth beneath the pit shaft, lay a rich vein, but this one was to make Ashington different from the many pit towns of the North East. Not coal gold this, but a family which was to dominate football, the passion of the working classes on a Saturday afternoon.

The Milburn Clan were to light up our national sport and none more so than Jackie Milburn, a miner's son who escaped the lung bursting coal dust for soccer immortality.

He first saw the light of day on May 11, 1924 in the upstairs flat of his grandparents' home at 14, Sixth Row, Ashington. From the bedroom window you could see the pityard and the shaft leading down to the coalface. The new bouncing baby was christened John Edward Thompson after his mother's father — the initials, JET, eagerly pounced on by sports-writers in later years when his speed made him one of the most feared centre-forwards in the land.

Jackie recalled his early days thus: 'It was a familiar view in the North East in the mid-twenties and one which drew most of the

Wor Jackie's grandfather Jack Milburn (centre of back row), who used to be called the Old Warhorse.

lads like a magnet. The bit money that could be made down the pit — and the beer it could buy — spoilt many a promising football career. Certainly it prevented my dad, Alec Milburn, from making the big time. He could have gone to Tottenham Hotspur but preferred to stay home and drink his ale.'

Football, however, was in the Milburn blood. His great grandfather, Jack Milburn, used to play in goal for Northumberland before the turn of the century and his son, another Jack Milburn was known as Old Warhorse because he was one of the strongest full-backs in the county. Then there were cousins Jack Milburn (Leeds), George (Leeds and Chesterfield), Jim (Leeds) and Stan (Chesterfield and Leicester) plus their sister Cissie's two little lads, Bobby and Jack Charlton, who grew up to be World Cup winners.

Right from the start young Jackie lived for football. At school he played left-back or outside-right and once, disastrously, at centre-forward. In the schoolyard Jackie and his pals used to sing a song which went: 'Do you ken Hughie Gallacher the wee Scots lad, the best centre-forward Newcastle ever had.' In those days Gallacher was a hero, a little darting leader who was immortalised as a member of Scotland's Wembley Wizards. A scorer of thunderous goals, he led United to the First Division championship in 1927 . . . little did the three-year-old bairn in the Ashington pit rows know at the time he was later to wear Hughie's famed No. 9 shirt at Newcastle with such distinction.

Twenty-two houses made up Sixth Row in Ashington with 40 lads all of around the same age as Jackie. It was a haven for a young boy with dreams and when his mam and dad eventually found a house on the other side of the town Jack stayed on with his granny so that he could continue to play football with his mates.

By the time he was six years old and attending Hirst North School he was kicking out a pair of shoes a fortnight — hardly ideal for folk brought up without too many pennies in their pocket but Jackie remembered the pride in his dad's voice one day when he declared: 'He seems to be improving. He's kicking more with his left foot. Both shoes have gone!'

There was no organised football for the young siblings in Ashington but that didn't stem the enthusiasm. Jack would rise at 6.30 in the morning, gulp down breakfast, and play football with the lads from half past seven until half past eight. Then he would run the two miles to school, at lunch time hurry home for a quick meal and afterwards play still more football until school re-opened.

At night it was the same old routine. Swallow tea as quickly as possible and adjourn to the back lane where any old rag ball would suffice. With coats for goalposts they were in their heaven, the cobbled streets a paradise as in their minds they played at the great stadiums before thousands of fans. Practise meant kicking the ball against the outside nettie door and Jackie would recall: 'I never missed once.'

It also meant kicking a stone to and from school — eight miles a day — and he kept the same stone for three years until it was worn shiny and round. That type of blinkered dedication spawned many a football star between the wars when, against a backcloth of comparative poverty, there were no distractions to lure away budding footballers. Today's youth may have television and video games and holidays abroad with the family but Jackie had his stone and the nettie door!

Tanner Milburn, the brother of Wor Jackie's father and dad of Football League players Jack, George, Jim and Stan Milburn as well as daughter Cissie, whose two sons Bobby and Jackie Charlton went on to play for England.

While he remained at his granny's in Sixth Row he always spent Christmas with his mam and dad across Ashington and by the time he was eight he was to receive his first pair of new football boots for those weekend games in the People's Park. Before that he'd played in a pair of hand-me-downs from Willie Chambers, a next door neighbour, who was a year younger but had tremendously large feet.

'The Chambers had four elder brothers at work and could afford to buy football boots for Willie,' explained Milburn.

This particular Christmas Jack had asked for a pair of boots (nothing unusual in that) and a torch, which was something of a surprise. At 3a.m. on a bible black Christmas morning little Jackie cautiously crept out of bed to discover his brand new boots. He quickly laced them on, grabbed the torch, and ran half a mile to where his pals had gathered with a football pitch, floodlit by the torches of course, lying in wait.

'Honest, I just stood and cried my eyes out,' Jack said. 'My Christmas was shattered.' He couldn't get a game, you see. The teams were already made up!

The earliest sign of the greatness to come was Jackie's speed. He could outstrip the rest of the lads and he turned it to his monetary advantage. Whenever the neighbours wanted an errand run they would look out of their front door, spot Jack playing football with his mates, and call: 'Hey, Jack, would you like to run a message for me?' Those errands brought a penny a time, which was good dough for a boy from the pit rows.

One of his idols was Cyril Brown, who played for Glentoran and later for Sunderland and Brentford and when Cyril used to return to Ashington in the close season he would organise races amongst the kids to fill in the long summer vacations.

'The first prize I ever won was a box of paints for being the first lad home in a race around the block.'

Milburn's most endearing quality as a star was his modesty. For him there was no crowing over Wembley appearances or England caps, no self confidence which declared: 'I'm the greatest,' more a wide-eyed wonderment that life had been so good to him. It stemmed, he always insisted, from a massive inferiority complex instilled in him as a boy and traceable to a particular sports day at school.

'I had won the 80 yards, long and high jump, and been a member of the winning relay team when my father arrived in the ground to see me take part in, and win, the 440 yards. Immediately I crossed the finishing line I fell flat on my face, having taken part in too many events and being worn out. For all that I wasn't prepared for the reception I got from my dad. "What's the matter with you?' he asked. 'Got a big head?"

'Dad proceeded to give me a good hiding to make sure I kept my feet on the ground in the future. His intentions, I'm certain, were the best in the world but that hiding laid the foundations for an inferiority complex which I always found difficult to overcome.'

Though football scouts were never to beat a path to Milburn's door a major step in the right direction came at the age of 12 when he was selected to play at outside right for Hirst East Senior Boys School. It was his first 'honour' and it sent the adrenalin racing.

'Won't dad be delighted?' enthused a young Jackie to his mam. 'Can I stay up to tell him?'

Dad, a coal cutter at the local pit, was on night shift but Jack lay in bed until he heard him come home at 1.30 in the morning only for his bottle to fail him. He decided against getting up to impart his good news but, unable to sleep, finally slipped down stairs to put on his red and green football shirt, blue shorts, and football

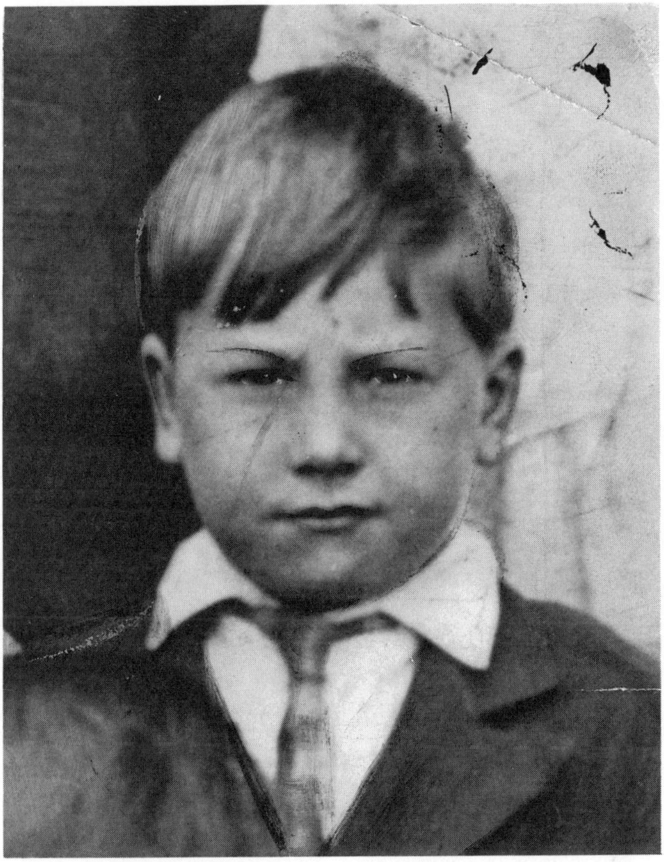

Jackie Milburn at the age of eight in 1932.

boots and sit in front of the slowly dying coal fire wishing away the hours until the kick off against Linton School.

An excited Milburn was at the ground a full two hours before the 10 o'clock start with his father, mother and two sisters, Jean and Mavis, finally coming along in support.

'Now, son,' said dad just before the kick-off, 'I want you to give a good account of yourself. You'll get a penny for every goal you score.'

Milburn duly scored twice as his team scorched to a 6-4 win and a proud youngster went home in a daze proudly clutching tuppence in his sweaty hand. Not even a Cup winner's medal could ever surpass that first feeling of triumph.

Jack's schoolboy career blossomed with Hirst East Boys winning

Early success — Jackie, second from the right in front row, pictured with the Hirst East schools side which won the league championship in 1937-38. Back row (left to right): Mr Wood, B. Thirtle, G. Bird, B. Jacques, R. Ryder, J. Harker, W. Ponton, Mr Garbutt, Mr Ford. Front row: D. Freeman, T. Mackie, A. Jackson, Jackie Milburn, Jim Milburn.

the local league championship in season 1937-38 and his selection for East Northumberland in the English Schools Shield when they went on to reach the semi-final and played at Maine Road, the home of the famous Manchester City where he was later to star in so many epics as a Football League player.

Lancashire beat East North 3-2 but Jackie scored one of the goals and proudly carried the clipping from the *Newcastle Football Chronicle* for years to come.

His inside-forward in that match was a close mate Joss Gray, who still lives in Ashington to this day, as do so many of his schoolboy friends. Ashington folk have deep roots.

Joss was a grand player, who was also captain of Northumberland and had three international trials. He later signed amateur forms for Sunderland and played in the same ATC side as Jack during the war.

'We never got away in those days but when we played at Maine Road we stayed in a big posh hotel overnight,' said Josh. 'I

Stan Milburn, who went on to play for Chesterfield and Leicester pictured with his sister Gladys.

remember Jackie and the rest of the lads playing snooker on the eve of the game in the hotel.

'Lancashire were three goals up at half-time but we were all over them in the second-half and pulled back to 3-2 with Jackie scoring one of our goals. If we'd got them back to Portland Park in Ashington we'd have done them all right but they went on to lift the trophy.

'Jackie was fast but he wasn't exceptional at the time. He wasn't a ball player. There were better lads on our side.'

All his old mates tell the same tale. Jack was mustard keen but steady rather than spectacular. Though when it came to races round the back streets as one told me: 'It wasn't worth us taking part. There was nee point — he was far too quick for us.'

Jackie's headmaster in those formative years was Jack Denton, who always used to tell him: 'Toes down, heel up and you'll score.' After that piece of simple advice brought him two goals at Wembley in the 1951 F.A. Cup final Milburn, never one to forget old friends, not only invited Mr Denton to attend a reception given him at Ashington's Methodist Central Hall but reserved him a place on the main platform where his former headmaster took an embarrassed ovation from the audience.

Lessons are learned early in life and Jackie's education took a significant turn when he attended his first big football match.

'I was only 13 and Billy Clark, a well known local boxer, took me to a game at Roker Park,' Milburn told me years later. 'When Raich Carter ran out he looked immaculate, hair slicked perfectly into shape and stockings showing precisely the right number of inches of white turn-over. "If you ever want to be a professional footballer you must look like him," Billy told me. Much later Carter emphasised the point when he said to me: "If you don't look the part you'll never be the part.' I never forgot that." '

CHAPTER TWO

Down the Pit

The pit inevitably beckoned as manhood approached. After all, where else was there to go in Ashington? While pit folk are the salt of the earth, burrowing your way underground past the pit props, choking on coal dust with only the light from your lamp to cast eerie shadows on the low ceiling hardly appealed to Jackie Milburn as he prepared to leave Bothel School where he had switched in 1938.

He wanted the open air life but where and how was the difficulty. The North East was in depression — just two years previously two hundred men with starving families had taken up their banners and walked for 26 days to reach London in an act which was to go down in history as the Jarrow hunger march. Adolf Hitler was already in power in Germany and a destructive, inhuman war lay a matter of months away, but to Milburn it was time to act and to broaden his horizons beyond the 10-mile limit of Ashington.

The South, where the grass seemed greener and the sun brighter, beckoned invitingly and a home bird was about to fly the coop. A pal named Eddie Main had got a job as a pantry boy and he supplied Jackie with the name and address of an agent in Ashington who specialised in sending youngsters to the more affluent South.

Yes, young Jack could be fixed up. A Captain Evelyn, who owned a large house at Dorking in Surrey, needed household staff and Milburn, too, could become a pantry boy just like Eddie.

Going into service and worse, leaving home, brought tears to the eyes of a mother about to lose her son but at seven o'clock on the following Saturday evening early in August Jackie packed his little bag ready for the journey into the unknown. Spare suit, shirt, underclothes, toothbrush but no shaving gear . . . the fresh faced boy was only 14 and had no need for such things.

Going down the pits or going south were the two main options for Ashington teenagers and another pal, Lance Richardson, was also travelling to London to join Fred Darling's Beckhampton stable as an apprentice jockey. It was a comfort but as the bus left the River Tyne behind it to bury its way down country the feeling of excitement and adventure was replaced by apprehension and fear. Every mile which took Jackie farther away from Ashington only added to the foreboding.

Dorking was a charming place, the house like a mansion after the colliery houses of the North East but it wasn't home. Oh sure, Jack's room was comfortable and his boss pleasant but the love of a closely knit family — and the football — were missing. It took Jackie only a matter of hours to pack again and run away.

With his heart pounding and the apprehension of a thief escaping the scene of the crime Milburn headed up the road with nowhere particular in mind, just to get as far away as possible. Two miles he had travelled when a large car purred up beside him and the Captain alighted. He'd heard Jackie leave the house and had given chase. A few kind words and a red faced youngster was driven back to spend the rest of the day washing dishes and cleaning silver feeling totally ashamed of himself.

It was only to be a temporary return, however. Home sickness gnawed away at Jackie's stomach and breaking point came when he was given a few hours off and went into Dorking to watch a football match. Instead of making him feel more settled it reminded him of the pleasures of playing the game he loved back in the North East.

'The following day I counted my few shillings, boarded the train for London, and wondered just where it would all end. It was at Waterloo Station, when I got off the train, that I made my big decision. I decided to forget my pride and call on my Auntie Isabella who lived in Eton Mews. So with only one shilling and

The Ashington ATC team with 16-year-old Jackie Milburn second from the left on the front row.

sixpence in my pocket I hired a taxi and was driven to my aunt's place. She gave me the money for my fare home and on the Wednesday night I was walking along Ashington's main street not quite sure whether I was happy, disappointed, or downright ashamed of myself.'

The guilt was eased somewhat when Jack's eyes alighted on a message scrawled in chalk on a wall: 'Welcome back, Gordon.' His pal and fellow adventurer Lance Richardson had also got homesick and returned to Ashington two days earlier.

Wrapped in the security of home life again was fine but a young man must do something to earn a few shillings and his gaze turned to the pit heaps. What else? Jackie decided to become an apprentice fitter at the colliery but, with no immediate vacancies, he was forced to turn to an alternative — working in a store weighing sugar and carrying round bags of flour.

It wasn't ideal but it filled in the three months until he at last landed a job in the saddler's shop at the pit making knee pads and belts and oiling the harnesses for the pit ponies which worked beneath the ground. In those days young lads had to join the pit before the age of 16 and serve a five-year apprenticeship and Milburn had made it in time.

Football consisted of playing locally wherever he could. For a time he assisted Hirst East Old Boys, who had a useful side, and then played in the Ashington Midget League with a new team formed by a group of pals. They were a disaster with scores regularly making double figures.

The outbreak of war in 1939 changed things considerably. The men folk either joined up or, if they were in the pits, served in the Air Training Corps, the home guard or the like. Joss Gray came home from Roker Park and joined the ATC as did Jackie, still only 15. He was not yet the strapping centre-foward who was to become a footballing legend — he was knee high to a grasshopper, a mere 5ft 0¼in and had been turned down by the Royal Navy because he was half an inch below the standard required. So it was the ATC for our young hero . . . and more football.

Four nights a week he trained on the Ashington Recreation Ground after putting in a tough spell in the gym. Then it was a hectic free-for-all match often with as many as 20 lads on each side with trees acting as the goalposts. Money was tight, people were skint but happy, and more often than not the youngsters would play in their pit boots or even with a piece of wood, shaped like a shoe, held on by string.

James Morton, who played as an amateur for Stockton, Ashington and the famous Scottish club Queen's Park, ran the ATC team and as a sprightly 83-year-old living in Rottingdean near Brighton remembers: 'Jackie first came to my notice when I was chief engineer of the Ashington Coal Company. He applied for an apprenticeship and was employed as an apprentice mechanic.

'Later as the officer and then commanding officer of 1010 ATC Squadron Jack came under my training in the squadron football team and he was a member of the 1010 Ashington Squadron ATC team that won the Northern Command Cup in 1941.

'He was a fine player but, surprising as it may seem, at that time he wasn't as good as some of the other boys in the side.'

Nevertheless now playing at outside-right or inside-right Jackie's performances for Ashington ATC were good enough for him to be selected for the Northumberland county team to play Yorkshire at Redheugh Park, the home of Gateshead when they

Back to his roots — Jackie pictured in 1988 with some of the miners at his old pit Ashington Colliery when it closed down.

were a Football League club. Northumberland won 3-0 and Wilf Taylor, then a Newcastle United director, invited all the players to watch Newcastle play Darlington.

Cyril Brown, back home and down the pits with the war in full flight, was guesting for Darlington and the thought of a first ever trip to St. James's Park delighted Milburn. It was big time, exciting, and an eager Jackie travelled with one of his pals, left-half Ray Poxton, to 'the toon' on the afternoon. But expectatons quickly evaporated — the match was grim with little skilful football and the two aspiring footballers began to think that they could do better. On the bus home to Ashington they could talk of little else and by the time they were walking down the colliery row they had decided to answer the annual advertisement for trials United put in the *North Mail* before the start of a new season.

It was the dawn of the 1943-44 season and Jackie was now 19. He had grown — my, how he had grown: as much an nine inches in nine months — and his big breakthrough lay immediately in front of him. Not that he realised it.

Raymond was a mining student with neat, impressive handwriting and it was decided he should pen the crucial letter composed by the pair of them. Five days later came the reply from Newcastle secretary Frank Watt asking them to report to St. James's Park at two o'clock the following Saturday complete with boots. It was just like Christmas, only better. Neither of them could wait until it was time to open their present and they arrived at the deserted ground fully four hours too early. It was pouring with rain as they sat lost on the steps leading up to the entrance and, unsure of what to do, they decided to go off to a local cafe where they each tucked in to a couple of meat pies — hardly the ideal preparation for players just before the kick-off.

Football in the 40s had none of the trappings of today's game. There were no glamour pre-season friendlies, no visiting foreign sides upon which to sharpen and refine your skills. Public matches consisted of The First Team v The Rest or The Probables v The Possibles. A lot of the top players were away fighting the war but there was still Albert Stubbins, a ginger haired centre-forward with awesome speed who rattled in an unbelievable 245 wartime goals, Scottish international Jimmy Gordon and left-half Duggie Wright, on leave from the Army.

Jack sat out the first-half of the trial and watched as a lad called Steve Howden, playing inside-left, which was to be his position in the final 45 minutes, scored two goals. The challenge was laid down.

Years afterwards Jackie, in total modesty, described what happened in the second-half.

'I was fortunate to have with me in my left wing triangle two experienced players in left winger Charlie Woollett and left-half Bobby Jacques. These two fine players prompted me all the time. Everything I attempted hit the jackpot and I scored two goals.

'It was different for Ray Poxton. He played with two young lads like him struggling to make the grade and he never had a chance. It just goes to prove that luck plays a vital part in football.'

As he came off the field Stan Seymour, a man whose influence went way beyond the boardroom, invited Milburn to return the following week for another trial. For Poxton there was no such offer and a dream was cruelly wrecked. Ray went on to have trials

The famous Milburn clan all together. From left to right sitting: George Milburn, Jack Milburn, Jackie Milburn, Bob and Cissie Charlton, Jackie Charlton, Bobby Charlton. Standing at the back are Jim Milburn and Stan Milburn.

at Darlington but never made the big step over the threshold, though in his own way he had gained a sort of immortality as the lad who went for a trial to Newcastle with the great Jackie Milburn.

Jack was always very conscious of the fact that he was lucky and other people might have done the same as him had they been given the same opportunities. Joss Gray recalls years after his glittering career was over bumping into Wor Jackie in the Ashington streets. Jack turned to Joss's missus and said: 'You know, he should have been famous instead of me,' to which she replied: 'Aye, but we mightn't have got married if that had happened.'

Pit life came before football and Milburn worked his shift at the colliery until 12 noon before his second trial match. Superstition played a big part in his young life and so it was back to the same cafe for another two pies as a pre-match meal. In those days

Milburn used to play with a white handkerchief tightly clenched in one of his fists. Why no one seems quite sure, though it was ventured that he was merely taking things a step further. Players often had a handkerchief tucked up the long sleeve of their shirt anyway.

'None of us exactly knew why Jackie carried that handkerchief,' one of his long-time mates told me, 'but he certainly didn't seem to play as well without it. It took him quite a while to get out of the habit.'

This time Milburn was to start the game wearing the famous black and white stripes of Newcastle against The Blues. Once more, he was linked up with Woollett and Jacques but things didn't quite click as before. By half-time Jackie's side were three goals down and Stubbins had scored twice.

Joe Richardson, a full-back who was to spend almost half a century in service at St. James's, was one of the trainers. Perhaps he felt a certain sympathy for the Ashington pit lad coming as he did from nearby Bedlington and he pulled him to one side in the interval.

'You better buck up your ideas, son, if you want to come here,' he told Jackie, who had let self doubt creep in as the first-half unfolded.

It was now time for a gambler's throw and Milburn, playing through the middle, went wild. With the ball constantly fed through quickly for him to make runs from almost the halfway line, using his great pace, he scored no fewer than six goals as his side rattled in nine.

At the finish Tot Smith, a robust centre-half, told a delirious Milburn: 'I've played here a long time but that's the biggest roasting I've ever had.'

The Sunday Sun described Jackie as 'a tall youth who showed a great capacity for quick attack and opportunism who, with training, could have a bright future.'

Seymour, that master signer, had no doubts. He implored Milburn to sign professional forms there and then and promised him a place in the first team the following week. To most that would be a dream come true but the only problem was that Jackie had promised his dad he would sign no forms before he and his uncle Tanner — father of Leeds United full-backs George and Jack Milburn — had seen them. It was a problem, a real problem. United had unearthed a gold nugget but if a six-goal forward was allowed to leave the ground unprotected another Football League club might just get wind of it and move in. A compromise was reached — Milburn would sign an amateur form and return 48 hours later on the Monday with his father Alec to become a pro.

'As soon as we entered his office Stan Seymour slid his arm round my dad's shoulder and led him towards the desk saying: 'Come on, Alec. Let's have a drink.' Out came the whisky bottle and before long dad was pie-eyed. He'd always been a great Newcastle United fan and Stan had been his hero on the left wing. This was like meeting the Prime Minister.

'I was sitting in a chair immediately behind Stan when I suddenly noticed that he had his hand behind his back. In it were two five pound notes — my signing on fee — and he fingered them like a magician fanning out a pack of cards. I'd never seen so much money in my life and I was mesmerised. I couldn't sign quick enough.'

Milburn put pen to paper for thirty shillings a match plus expenses to and from the ground — 'purely a wartime measure,' insisted Seymour. 'When League football is resumed you can leave your job in the pit to become a full-time professional and your wages will be very much higher.'

On the bus home Jackie worked out how to spend his tenner . . . five pounds for his mam to buy a new dress, a pound for his dad to get a pint or two and some tobacco, and four pounds for himself to get a much needed new suit. Heady times!

CHAPTER THREE

Early Days with United

Stan Seymour became known as Mr Newcastle and rightly so. His record with the club was outstanding both as a player and a director. He was a down-to-earth man with no airs and graces and a Geordie accent you could cut with a knife. But, my, how he knew his football.

Seymour's background was similar to that of Jackie. Born in the little mining village of Kelloe in county Durham, by the age of 13 he had taken his first job collecting the tokens off the pit tubs at the local colliery. His path to St. James's Park had come via Bradford City and, unusually for an English player in those days, Greenock Morton in Scotland where he stayed for seven happy years.

At Newcastle the little outside-left became a star scoring in the 1924 F.A. Cup winning side against Aston Villa — only the second year the final had been staged at Wembley — and then starring in the same forward line as the immortal Hughie Gallacher which won the First Division championship in 1927. Two years later he left United amid much bitterness and for a time wasn't welcome within the great portals of St. James's until, with the black and whites at their lowest ebb in 1938 just before the outbreak of war, he was unexpectedly offered a seat on the board.

Instead of waiting for the pre-war players to return as veterans as some clubs did the shrewd Seymour searched the area for young talent and groomed them in readiness for the resumption

Wor Jackie's early hero at St. James's Park, Albert Stubbins.

of the Football League. In 1941 Charlie Wayman arrived from Chilton Colliery and Tommy Walker from Esh Winning; in 1942 it was little Ernie Taylor (Sunderland); 1943 saw Bobby Cowell (Trimdon Grange) and Jackie Milburn (Ashington); and 1944 brought in Charlie Crowe (Walker). They were followed by bargain buys and United were on the path to success.

Few have ever equalled Seymour's record as a talent spotter. He could find a diamond amongst the pebbles on the beach but he always maintained that Wor Jackie was his best ever capture.

'I got him for ten quid and he became priceless,' said Stan. 'What made Milburn was that he wasn't just an outstanding footballer but a fine sportsman into the bargain. He was the perfect example to the younger generation.'

Jackie had been promised an immediate first team place after his six-goal performance and it came on August 28, 1943 at Bradford City.

Seymour's stamp was always to do things first class. He knew successful teams had good players and looked after them, and that was to be his unerring line throughout his days of power at St. James's. Even in war-time football Seymour practised what he preached and he told Jackie: 'Bring your dad to Bradford. All expenses will be paid by the club — and to make sure you don't miss the train the pair of you can spend the Friday night in the County Hotel.'

To pit folk it was the equivalent of being told you were dossing in Buckingham Palace. Alec Milburn had never even stayed in an hotel before — he didn't even drink in the saloon bar at the local club because of the cost, so this was really living.

'We sat up until one o'clock in the morning talking and smoking,' Jackie told me. 'We were in bed little more than a couple of hours before. Too excited to sleep, we got up, opened the window and sat gazing out over the sombre, grey station forecourt as the dawn broke through.

'Before we boarded the eight o'clock train I met the rest of the players underneath the big clock in the Central Station. A lot of players used to guest for clubs during the war and I remember Jimmy Mullen, later of Wolves and England fame who was to partner me at inside-left, and Billy Nicholson, who later played right-half for Spurs and England.'

United lost 2-1 with City's inside-right scoring both their goals. His name: Joe Harvey, who only a few short years on was to captain Wor Jackie twice at Wembley.

'I didn't play too well. I missed a couple of easy chances with my head but Stan Seymour still patted me on the back at the end of the game and said: "Well played, son. You'll be in the side again next week." I was grateful for that.'

Bradford were at St. James's in a return just seven days later and within two minutes of his home debut Milburn scored with a left foot shot from 10 yards out at the Leazes end. United won 3-2.

Jack, still a pit lad, was learning his new profession while the defeat of Hitler was still being completed but his progress had picked up momentum and was recognised by perhaps the greatest of them all, Stanley Matthews.

United crushed Stoke City 9-1 early in the 1945-46 season with

Len Shackleton, his mate at Hazlerigg Colliery who scored six goals on his debut for United.

local boys Bobby Corbett and Charlie Crowe blotting out the magical Matthews. Everyone was pretty chuffed back in the dressing-room when suddenly there was a tap on the door.

Matthews stuck his head round and asked for Jackie. On being introduced he said: 'I watched you this afternoon and you've got a bright future in the game if you keep playing like that.'

Playing like that is something Milburn obviously did because in years still to come he and Matthews would wear the white shirt of England together.

Jack's pace and some inferior defending, with many top class players away, fleetingly lifted the clouds of savage confrontation in Europe. United's wartime guests included Sunderland winger

Len Duns over the first three seasons; Tom Finney in 1942-43 (three goals in six games); Manchester United's Allenby Chilton (two matches); and a single appearance by Stan Mortensen, as well as Jimmy Mullen (15 games and 4 goals) and Bill Nicholson (19 matches).

Wor Jackie's personal record was: 1943-44 — 24 games and 12 goals; 1944-45 — 32 matches and 12 goals; and 1945-46 — 39 games and 14 goals.

In each of his seasons United's top scorer was Albert Stubbins, who brought a cascade of goals. Albert wore size 11 boots and packed a fearsome shot. Capped in a wartime international in 1945, he once scored no fewer than four hat-tricks in succession.

Season 1946-47 saw the resumption of League football. United were still a Second Division side after going down in 1934, but Seymour the local talent spotter had also got out the cheque book to buy in the best. Joe Harvey had arrived from Bradford City for £4,250; Roy Bentley, a debonair inside-forward, came from Bristol City for £8,500; and a mountain of a centre-half called Frank Brennan cost £7,500 from Scottish club Airdrie.

As the bad memories of a horrendous war were put behind us United opened their new campaign at Millwall with a mixture of the old and the new. The forward line consisted of a youthful Jackie Milburn partnered by Roy Bentley with that wartime goal machine Albert Stubbins at centre-forward, local lad Charlie Wayman inside-left and Tommy Pearson, now well into his 30s but about to gain two Scottish caps, on the left wing.

A crowd of 39,187 turned up to welcome back the chase for promotion points and United cruised home 4-1 with Bentley hitting a couple, Wor Jackie one and Stubbins the other.

It was all a new experience to Jackie. 'When we arrived at our London hotel the previous night there'd been a mix-up and instead of a double and single bed in our room there was only one double. So I slept between new signings Frank Brennan and Roy Bentley in the double bed and never got a wink of sleep. They snored like troopers.

'The next morning Roy, who knew London well, said he'd show us around and off we went for a walk. The only trouble was that we lost him in the seething London crowds. The game was only a

A young Jackie Milburn enjoys a cigarette. He was to smoke them at half-time in the Wembley dressing-room.

couple of hours away and we didn't know where we were — Frank fresh down from Scotland and me an Ashington pit lad. So, to make certain we didn't get split up, Frank and I held hands as we pushed our way through the Saturday morning shoppers looking for a tube station to get us back to our hotel. We must have looked a couple of right nancy boys — two six-foot footballers holding hands!'

Seymour the wheeler dealer wasn't finished. In little more than a month two significant transfers — one in and one out — were to be completed. Stubbins, in many ways a model of Milburn with his modesty, blistering speed and goalscoring opportunism, asked for a transfer. The interest was enormous but in the end it boiled down to two clubs, Everton and Liverpool.

Liverpool's boss George Kay was at Gallowgate while Seymour had Everton manager Theo Kelly at the Royal Station Hotel communicating by telephone. Both were astutely played off against one another as the bidding went up £1,000 a time until Liverpool eventually won the day at £13,000.

The money went straight to Bradford to bring in an inside-forward called Len Shackleton, a ball-playing genius who became known as the Clown Prince of Soccer because of his cheeky style.

The crowds had come flocking back as United opened with a six-match unbeaten run . . . 54,966 for the first home League game with Swansea (1-1) and 55,313 the following Wednesday when Coventry were beaten 3-1 at St. James's Park. Even the first defeat, at home to Burnley 2-1, saw 61,255 packing the park. Unbelievable crowds in the Second Division.

But the real drama was still to come on Shack's debut. The date, October 5, 1946 — a game which was to be written into the annals of United's history.

Newport County, who had lost their previous game by seven goals to West Bromwich Albion, were the opposition as 52,137 turned up to see the new boy's first game without realising the treat which was in store.

United fielded the following team: Garbutt; Cowell, Graham; Harvey, Brennan, Wright; Milburn, Bentley, Wayman, Shackleton, Pearson.

Within 90 seconds Charlie Wayman had missed a penalty but Shackleton soon started the massacre, laying on a far post cross for Wayman to head home. Two minutes later Shack beat three men to take a return pass and score his first. Wayman netted twice more in two minutes, both goals created by Shackleton, to complete a hat-trick inside half an hour. Did rain ever fall quicker?

Within the space of eight incredible minutes United scored five goals including a Shack hat-trick within five of those minutes to lead by an astonishing 7-0 at half-time.

With former England wing-half Doug Wright running the midfield United refused to take their foot off the accelerator and poor Turner in the Newport goal was shell-shocked. After the interval Shackleton was on the mark again, Milburn hit two, and in the 73rd minute Wayman netted his fourth before Bentley got in on the act to make it 12-0.

United's thirteenth was credited to Shack but by now Newport didn't know what time of day it was and the ball actually went into the net off Wookey. By the time the final whistle blew the scoreline read Newcastle United 13, Newport County 0, and record after record had been smashed . . . it's still the biggest ever win in the club's history and smashed the Second Division record of the day. Shack's six goals was the best ever debut and his second, third and fourth goals the fastest hat-trick scored by an individual.

Never before had a single player made such an impact. Shack was a magician, shaking his hips to send befuddled defenders the wrong way and bending the ball with a nonchalant flick of his educated feet. He was a sorcerer, one of the game's quickest thinkers who would play the ball off the corner flag to beat an opponent or even sit on the ball in the heat of play to get a belly laugh from the crowd.

'Shack was the greatest ball player of all time,' maintained Milburn. 'He could balance a ball on a snowflake. He was a born entertainer, always original and intentive. Len never knew what he was going to do next so what chance did we mere mortals have?

'He never forgave Arsenal for turning him down as a kid and whenever we were playing in London he wouldn't train with us that week. He'd be off on his own practising his party pieces. He was determined to grab the headlines every time we played in the capital and came up with one original trick after another.'

By now Jackie was working as a fitter at Hazlerigg Colliery and United got Shack a job as his labourer.

'It's hard to think of the highly skilled and artistic Shackleton being skivvy to anyone but these were difficult times and when it came to football we were still semi-pro. We had a lot of fun together — I had a motorbike even though they were banned by the club because they were too dangerous and we used to roar round the countryside on it thoroughly enjoying ourselves.

'We even rode on the bike to St. James's Park every Tuesday and Thursday morning for training, stashing it round the back out of sight and walking into the ground. If the club had known two such valuable assets were risking their necks at least twice a week they would have gone spare.'

Jackie had moved from Ashington Colliery across town to Woodhorn and then, with the help of Newcastle United, to

Hazlerigg. United's directors had a pull with the Hazlerigg bosses when it came to Jackie getting time off to play football and they even arranged for him to see a doctor who diagnosed slight ear trouble which helped to make life a little easier. The pits were a reserved occupation during the war which meant Jack and other pitmen were exempt from joining the forces but also meant, of course, he couldn't become a full-time footballer.

His mates recalled his time at the collieries as one obsessed by football.

'The wall outside the fitting shop at Ashington pit was whitewashed and covered in dirty marks where Jackie kicked a ball against it,' one told me. 'I'd have loved to have had a tanner for every mark on that wall.

'The Recreation Ground was just next door and whenever Jackie could get away he'd organise a game of football even when he was playing for Newcastle's first team. Often there would be up to 20 a side and of course everyone wanted to have a go at Jackie, because he was the star. They wanted to blot him out of the game but he'd just take the hard tackles no bother.'

Les Common, who was six years younger than Jackie and spent 21 years down the pits at Ashington, was spotted playing in local football by Jackie and actually signed amateur forms for 'the toon' as a result. He later became Jackie's brother-in-law, marrying his younger sister Mavis, but at the time Milburn had no idea the teenage winger was secretly seeing his sister.

'I remember the date to this day — January 20, 1947. I was playing outside-left for Linton Juniors and Jack sent for me. I went to see him in the Fourth Row at Ashington. He was sitting in a blue pullover and looked immaculate as always. 'I've had good reports about you and would like to take you through to St. James's Park,' he said in a quiet voice. Jack picked me up in a little Ford Eight motorcar and off we went. Newcastle signed no fewer than five players that night including goalkeeper Ray Wood, who later played for Manchester United. But I never made it big at Newcastle, going on to captain Tow Law in non-league football.'

Les, who married Mavis in the February of 1952, was a firm fan of Wor Jackie long before he became an official member of the Milburn clan.

'I used to get paid a penny for throwing coal into the coalhouse and saved it up to watch Newcastle play on the Saturday. It cost one shilling and tuppence there and back from Ashington, tenpence for a three course meal at the British Restaurant, sixpence to get into the match and a penny for a programme. Jack regularly played in his black pit socks with no white turnover.

'When he first arrived at Newcastle he learned from Harry Clifton, an inside-left from Newburn. Harry could hold the ball up beautifully but I think that the player who really made Jack was Len Shackleton. You could see Shack making Jackie think. He was the icing on the cake.'

Milburn maintained: 'Before the start of the golden era which was to see us promoted to the First Division and win the F.A. Cup three times in five years there was one final lesson still to be learned. It came in the 1946-47 season when we reached the semi-final of the Cup and took on Charlton Athletic at Leeds. The rumblings in the camp didn't augur well. Both Joe Harvey and Len Shackleton said before the game that they would never play for Newcastle United again because they had been promised a house by the club and hadn't got one. That was bad enough but when the manager George Martin dropped top scorer Charlie Wayman and put in George Stobbart at centre-forward the balloon went up.

'We got turned over badly 4-0 though Peter Croker kicked three shots off the line in the first 10 minutes before Don Welsh hit the goals trail. Suddenly we were failures and didn't like the feeling.

'That was the last time there was any real discontent in the club because we all learned from the Charlton debacle. The club learned that you cannot mess about the players and the players learned you can't mess about the supporters.'

United had beaten Crystal Palace 6-2 at home in the third round, then Southampton 3-1 at St. James's in round four with a Wayman hat-trick, drawn 1-1 at home to Leicester and beaten them 2-1 in the replay, and finally eliminated Sheffield United away 2-0 in the sixth round with Milburn notching a goal.

Ironically, Charlton had also had their pre-match worries. They had visited a factory at Harrogate and eaten some salmon sandwiches which had kept several players up all night. In fact their famous goalkeeper Sam Bartram played with a hot poultice strapped on his stomach but skipper Don Welsh ran the show, covering every blade of grass to such an extent that he collapsed in the dressing-room afterwards through exhaustion.

CHAPTER FOUR

Powderhall Sprinter

If football hadn't claimed Jackie Milburn, then he might have become a great athletics star. As a sprinter he burned up the grass; he was a natural with little or no organised training. But then sport came naturally. He played cricket locally, bowling right or left arm effortlessly, and later played the game out in Ireland when with Linfield. He was also a tennis player, enjoying a game with George Robledo during their halcyon days as the finest strike force in the First Division, and when age took him beyond the boundaries of such sports he enjoyed nothing more than an afternoon on the golf course.

Athletics, however, was his forte away from football. As a boy Jackie had learned sprinting with his mates Edwin Dodds and Tom Willis. 'One of the most bitter disappointments was that there was no club in the area for me to join and enjoy my athletics even more,' he said.

That initial speed impressed United in his first training spell at St. James's Park.

'Albert Stubbins, who was looked upon as a greyhound, invited me to train with him and when I opened up the throttle I managed to get my nose in front over 100 yards. Andy McCombie was obviously impressed and when I was in the bath he brought along first team trainer Norman Smith. 'He's going to be a surprise for you, Norman,' said McCombie. 'He's even faster than Albert Stubbins.'

'Norman wanted to see for himself how this hare from

Ashington performed. So I climbed out of the bath, dried myself, donned spikes, and gave a one-man show for his benefit. 'I like your style, Jackie,' said Smith, himself a noted sprinter in his younger days. 'Speed is an essential part of football. We'll make a player of you here.'

In the forties when money was tight professional athletics blossomed in the North East, the borders and Scotland and it was an automatic vehicle for Milburn. A sport rich in colour and romance, it was nevertheless riddled with, shall we say, dubious goings on.

Huge cash changed hands through the on-course bookies, competitors often ran under assumed names, and tricks were pulled by the athletes aimed at affecting their odds come the big race. Many a runner would go out with lead in his shoes or a huge belt strapped under his singlet full of lead pellets to hold him back in minor races so that he produced a 'bad' time and was eased in the handicap of the major event. If drug abuse is today's serious problem, then it was straight old-fashioned cheating during and after the war.

Pro athletics may now be clean but a blind eye was turned on the 'minor' indiscretions of the old timers. Yet somehow amongst the working folk who loved their sport and loved a flutter foot handicaps remained a fascination which couldn't be resisted.

Powderhall, run in Edinburgh, was and is still the jewel at the very centre of the crown. It was Wembley, the highlight of the calendar. Its fame spread way beyond our shores to as far away as America, Canada, South Africa and Australia. Runners would make the long pilgrimage purely to run in this most prestigious event in the middle of winter when sometimes sprinters couldn't see the tape for the snowstorms.

This wasn't the pussy-footing athletics of today run in beautiful sunshine in places like Nice, Oslo or Rome. This was he man stuff in the depths of a Scottish winter on New Year's Day.

The Powderhall has been going for more than one hundred years. Since 1870 to be precise, and men of considerable finance over the border would keep athletes in secret training compounds for more than six weeks all expenses paid in the hope of pulling off a huge betting coup. Though the two-day meeting covered many distances the blue riband, of course, was the Powderhall Sprint.

Ossie Oswald (right), the man who took Jackie Milburn to Edinburgh for the Powderhall sprint, pictured with one of his Powderhall winners, Eddie Poxton (centre) and Jack Dryden.

This, then, was the fascinating and exciting world in which Jackie Milburn, a local pedestrian, was to find himself. A young man of infinite speed who, it was said, would surely have become a Powderhall champion had he not opted for football in the end.

Ossie Oswald, Ashington born and bred, was a top Powderhall man. Four times he reached a Powderhall final — in the famed 100 yards in 1941, 1942 and 1943 and the 200 yards in 1945 — and afterwards trained some of the North East's great winners. It was Ossie, who worked at the same pit as engineer Milburn, who was a major influence on his brief flirtation with professional athletics' major event.

'I ran under the name O. Sword. Nearly all of us had assumed names,' Ossie told me. 'In certain professions, shall we say, they might have frowned on their members running for money so it was easier to keep your identity a secret.

'Albert Spence from Blyth, who won the Powderhall in 1947 and was one of its greatest competitors, was really called Grant. And one of my boys who won the crown in 1959, Loss of Ashington, was Eddie Poxton, whose uncle was Raymond, the same lad who went with Jackie Milburn to Newcastle for a soccer trial. So it went on.

'After I'd finished running I trained several athletes including 1959 winner Loss of Ashington and Charlie Harrison from Bedlington who won in 1962. I linked up with a bloke called Tommy Parker, who had been a Powderhall half miler and owned a big temperance hotel at Crieff in Perthshire. He and his partner Bob Forster were the money men who unearthed promising runners and kept them in preparation for up to a month and a half before the New Year's Day race.'

This was the stable which saw in Jackie a future star. He ran locally, as did his Newcastle United colleagues Tommy Walker and Frank Brennan, and indeed had won a handicap at Portland Park in his home town and also ran with distinction at the Morpeth Olympics, a premier meeting in the north dating back to 1873. Ossie liked the look of the young man with speed to burn and in the December of 1943 invited him to go up to Scotland to Parker's training camp. Jack had just finished a shift at the pit but, with nothing to lose, he boarded a train at Newcastle's Central Station with Ossie.

'When we got up there Jackie put on his pumps to race against myself and another Powderhall runner, Jimmy Wallace of Blackburn. He beat the pair of us and Tommy Parker couldn't believe his eyes. He pulled me to one side. 'Do you realise, Ossie, that this fella is quicker than the bloke I've got in the keep?' A runner called Dave Craven from Blaydon was up living off the fat of the land for six weeks and was odds on favourite to win the Powderhall that year but Milburn, up for the day and without any specialised training, was quicker than him.

'Jack had to go home straight away but Parker begged me to keep an eye on him. He'd only been a trial horse but Tommy told Jack: 'If you come with us next year you'll win Powderhall. There are only two certainties in life — death and you to win on New Year's Day.'

'Jack said okay but to make certain he didn't shoot off I even took his pumps off him.'

Milburn asked for them back — and got them — to enable him

100 YARDS POWDERHALL HANDICAP

Run on MONDAY, 3rd JANUARY 1944, at 11.15 a.m.

FIRST PRIZE, £80 and the POWDERHALL GOLD MEDAL

Second, £10. Third, £5. Fourth, £3.

10/- each to Winners of Heats competing in second ties who do not get a prize.

J. H. Mitchell, Letham	1
G. L. Moodie, Craigmillar	1½
H. Ellis, Rushden	1½
W. McFarlane, Glasgow	1½
C. Chatburn, Chatburn	2
E. M. Aldam, Edinburgh (E. A. Marshall)	2
C. Weaver, Llanhilleth	3
N. Taylor, Blyth	3
R. Weaver, Llanhilleth	3
A. S. Price (R.A.F.), Burntwood	3
A. E. Smith, Redditch	3
G. J. Jenkins, Rhondda	4
J. M. Halley, Kilmarnock	4
F. Hindley, Worksop	4
R. Roberts, Amble	4
J. Hillard, Leicester	4
G. Troth, Barrow	4
J. H. Clifford, Pentwynmawr	4
W. Anness, Clitheroe	4
E. Goodsir (E. G. Archibald), Edinburgh	4
T. Egan, Merthyr Tydfil	4½
W. Dunleavy, Hapton	4½
A. Sarsfield, Accrington	4½
F. W. Oakley, York	4½
G. Cross, Winterton	4½
A. H. Randall, Gorseinon	4½
E. H. Sampson, British Honduras	4½
J. Jenkins, Ashington	4½
G. Gall, Dundee	5
G. Anthony, Edinburgh	5
W. Lee, Caerphilly	5
G. Bromley, Wrexham	5
A. E. McGregor, Edinburgh	5
C. Keen, Burradon	5
T. Whalley, Nelson	5
B. Gall, Dundee	5
A. Morrison, Dechmont	5
F. Foley, Barrow	5
R. Bell, Hebburn	5
J. Riggins, Glasgow	5
W. Black, Dunfermline	5
T. Sinclair, Leeds	5
D. Campbell, Glasgow	5
H. Whittaker, Clitheroe	5
S. Mitchell, Carlisle	5
W. Nicholson, Barrow	5
C. Pears (Brown), Ashington	5
J. Fallon, Stoke	5
D. Clarke, Niddry	5
E. Stuart, Loanhead	5
R. Roberts, Bridgend	5
J. Millburn, Ashington	5
J. Taylor, Grange Villa	5½
H. Appleby, North Shields	5½
E. Batten, Barnsley	5½
J. M. Differ, Twechar	5½
G. D. Cameron, Alva	5½
G. Stein, Broxburn	5½
J. Robertson, Barrow	5½
D. Bell, Barrow	5½
A. Mitchell, Kelty	5½
J. Peden, Armadale	5½
K. Kenny, Ashington	—
J. Raeburn, Uphall	5½
A. Redpath, Pelton Fell	5½
A. F. McGhee, Edinburgh	5½
A. Mitchell, Ashington	5½
C. Mellen, Barrow	5½
B. Hooks, Cardenden	5½
R. H. Metcalfe, Richmond	5½
W. Theurer, Edinburgh	5½
D. Craven, Blaydon	5½
R. Brandon (A. McLeod), Edinburgh	5½
D. Cash, Edinburgh	5½
C. Cooper, Carlisle	5½
J. McLevy, Sheffield	5½
A. McLachlan, Blackburn	5½
R. Sands, Strathaven	5½
J. Wallace, Blackburn	5½
M. H. Davies, Pontypridd	5½
A. Livingstone, East Kilbride	5½
H. McIntyre, Motherwell	5½
J. O'Connor, Lochore	5½
J. Aitken, Harthill	5½
T. Owens, Trindon	5½
G. Dick, Parkhall	5½
J. Stoddart, Douglas Water	5½
J. Davie, Balerno	5½
G. W. Holdcroft, Stoke	5½
W. Raymond, Stockton	5½
F. Murray, Stockton	5½
D. Smith, Armadale	5½
J. Smithson, Hanley	5½
J. Welsh, Wishaw	5½
F. Wilson, Kirkintilloch	5½
W. Williams, Ashington	5½
J. H. Tiffin, Morpeth	6
J. Lawrie, Hopetoun	6
J. Jardine, Peebles	6
R. Hale, Ashington	6
H. Hamilton, Cowdenbeath	6
T. Adams, Galashiels	6
J. Luke, Forest Hall	6
W. Scales, Prestonpans	6
T. Thomas, Whinney Hill	6
J. Millar, Dollar	6
T. Lewis, Llandebie	6
A. McArthur, Queensferry	6
D. McArthur, Queensferry	6
J. B. Walker, St. Boswells	6
W. Simpson, Dunfermline	6
J. Macdonald, Alexandria	6
H. Mills, Junr., Barry	6
J. Allan, Leith	6
J. Spencer, Macclesfield	6
H. Holdroyd, Liversedge	6
S. Black, Morpeth	6
J. O'Neill, Horden	6
D. Hamilton, Armadale	6
D. C. MacIntyre, Edinburgh	6
J. Urquhart, Edinburgh	6
N. Pentland, Ashington	6
A. Pringle, Gorebridge	6
D. McAndrews, Hamilton	6
J. James, Ashington	6
W. Carr, Newcastle	6½
J. O'Donnell, Niddry	6½
J. Farrell, Caldercruix	6½
A. W. Lindsay, Ayr	6½
T. Murdoch, Edinburgh	6½
C. McCallum, Alexandria	6½
T. Braid, Glencraig	6½

Wor Jackie's name, spelt Millburn, in the Powderhall Handicap programme of January, 1944.

to run in a local event in which again without any formal athletic training he was just beaten on the tape in the final.

Jack was aware of the tricks pulled by the top money stars and obviously felt if you couldn't beat 'em then you may as well join 'em. Les Common smilingly recalls: 'Jack got changed by a tree, leaving his jacket and trousers in a neat pile underneath it. After qualifying he returned to his gear and took off a huge Army belt he'd had strapped under his running shirt. He needed to be slowed down because he was obviously flying and ran in the final without it.'

Oswald himself admits: 'I used to have a belt myself with pockets in it into which I'd put lead weights. It could weigh a ton and it 'pulled' me in the heats.'

Milburn had already entered the Powderhall sprint to be run at the beginning of January, 1944, paying his ten shilling entrance fee as an individual with no backing from the major sponsors such as Parker and, despite his football commitments with United, he ran in the heats. Not unnaturally, without any preparation or guidance, he didn't qualify for the final. An old newspaper clipping reveals that he was beaten in heat 12 by a former Powderhall winner C. Chatburn, one of only two runners who were behind Jack who was off five yards. Ironic, perhaps, that while runners went to great lengths to assume 'new identities' Milburn did not. Yet in the official Powderhall programme his name was mis-spelt, perhaps an unwanted cloak of secrecy. He appeared as J. Millburn.

Yesteryear's footballers were attracted to pro running. When Jackie first donned spikes in Edinburgh the sprint was won by J. Urquhart, who was in reality J. Allan, a reserve outside-left with Hearts and another winner was J.H. Mitchell of Letham whose real name was Harley, another reserve whom Liverpool fined £100 for taking time off to participate in the Powderhall.

Jack's defeat in the 1944 races was dismissed by Oswald and Parker. He was a rookie, no more, without any preparation and they knew they had a secret weapon who could be unleashed with devastating effect a year hence. With that in mind Ossie persuaded Milburn to spend a week in soccer's close season back at Parker's camp when further inspection could be made. It was

THE HEATS

Heat 8 — O. Oswald, Ashington (6½.)

Also ran:— J. Lawrie, Hopetoun (6); J. Dawson, Leith (14½); R. Thomson, Dumbarton (8½); J. O'Neill, Horden (6); N. Taylor, Blyth (3); T. Braid, Glencraig (6½.)
Betting — Evens, Oswald.
Won by inches. Time, 10 5-10 secs.

Heat 9 — C. Chatburn, Chatburn (2.)

Also ran:— H. Robertson, Musselburgh (7½); J. Millburn, Ashington (5); C. McLaren, Edinburgh (7½); D. Smith, Armadale (5½); E. W. Coulthard, Workington (10); F. Hindley, Worksop (4.)
Betting — Evens, Chatburn.
Won by a yard. Time, 10 7-10 secs.

Heat 10 — J. H. Mitchell, Letham (1.)

Also ran:— J. Pringle, Musselburgh (12); J. Farrell, Caldercruix (6½); T. Thomas Whinney Hill (6); A. W. Lindsay, Ayr (6½); W. Theurer, Edinburgh (5½); J. Hamilton, Cathcart (13); J. Wallace, Blackburn (5½.)
Betting — 3/1 on Mitchell.
Won by a yard. Time, 10 7-10 secs.

Results of the Powderhall won by Hearts reserve outside-left J. Allan with Jackie in heat no. 9.

seven days during which Jackie visited Loch Lomond and other beauty spots in a country of breathtaking natural beauty in between sessions on the track. At the end of it Parker was more convinced than ever that he had a potential winner on his hands. The next step was the dodgy one — persuading Jackie to go for the £80 first prize and gold medal which awaited every Powderhall sprint winner. Not to mention the thank you from a grateful gaffer like Parker who would present his winners with solid gold watch and chains.

Parker, who bet in thousands of pounds in the hungry forties when money was supposedly tight and eventually faced an inquiry from the taxman after a bookie friend went to prison, decided to take no chances. He headed for Ashington to 'put the arm' on his young protégé.

When he arrived unexpectedly Jackie was out with a girl. The next day Parker was more successful and they spoke frankly about Tommy's big plans, with Ossie adding fuel to the fire whenever necessary.

Milburn's imagination was fired but he lamented: 'If I run Powderhall Stan Seymour (his boss at United) has threatened to put me in the Army' — a reference to Jack's work at the pit which kept him out of the armed forces. Parker pointed out that United, paying poor wages in wartime, didn't rule Milburn's life and that he could 'produce the best doctors' to make certain Jack got time off to go into preparation.

Jackie, under pressure, agreed to talk to the directors at a board meeting to be held the next night. Parker, desperate not to let his man escape, decided to report to St. James's Park himself to lend his weight to the argument. But he sat for three hours without any sign of Milburn.

When Oswald inquired the next day why Jackie hadn't turned up he replied sheepishly: 'I've decided to stick with my football.'

Oswald, still a handicapper in professional athletics, maintains to this day: 'Jackie would have been a Powderhall champion without a shadow of doubt had he thrown in his lot with us. People like Walker and Brennan ran in local handicaps but they weren't fit to lace his shoes. He was a natural. He had it all and only needed proper training.'

That training would have meant living on the job, eating porridge and toast for breakfast, going on long morning walks, having poached egg for lunch, then down to serious training followed by a milk, egg and sherry drink before a slap up dinner with chump steaks an inch and a quarter thick. Andrew Hood, known to the runners as The Watcher, was a constant companion even if the boys went to the pictures.

Mitchell of Ashington — real name George Downs, an electrician at the local pit who won the 1946 sprint — was spirited away to Scotland for his preparation and said: 'They wouldn't even let me walk on the outside of the pavement in case I got knocked down.' Such was the investment in a Powderhall prospect. Dusty Downs, as he was known, was an Ashington pit lad who, like Wor Jackie, played for Newcastle United as a winger.

Milburn was to have one more go at Powderhall in a 'novice' capacity in 1945. And while his naive approach meant no big time glory he did win a 75 yards consolation race. Afterwards Jack, who merely travelled up to run and come straight back, went into a room and downed a jam sandwich. A German doctor, looking on, couldn't believe his eyes. 'No one can run that fast on a jam sandwich,' he lamented. 'This is nothing more than British propaganda!' I suppose in wartime a German could be excused for thinking we were pulling a fast one in producing our own master race.

Ronnie Coulson, who grew up with Milburn as a teenager in Ashington, accompanied him on one of his Powderhall trips.

'A few of us were going up to Edinburgh and we had lunch in a little cafe near Stan Seymour's shop in the Newcastle city centre. We went through the card . . . soup, rabbit, two veg, the lot. The only trouble was that they served it all at once. We tucked in as best we could but when it was time to get the train there was still plenty of rabbit left in the pot. So we wrapped it up in a copy of the *Evening Chronicle* and sat on the train doling out bits of rabbit to everyone in the compartment!

'It was hardly the way to approach a big run but Jack was inexperienced and when he went into a race more often than not it was to win. He would smash the clock which meant a stiffer handicap.'

What made Powderhall the most romantic of meetings was the time of year it was run and the rough and ready facilities. Runners didn't wear flashy tracksuits with sponsors' names emblazoned on them like today. Jack's tracksuit was an old goalie's jersey and a pair of old trousers. The athletes warmed up on a small footpath round the back of the changing rooms and on occasions as much as six inches of snow was swept off the track before runners went to their marks. Lanes were, and often still are, cordoned off by long pieces of wool over the 100 yards.

Neither Steve Cram, Steve Ovett nor Seb Coe have experienced such icy conditions as Scotland throws up at Hogmanay. Competitors often had to literally dig holes at the start to gain a hold with their spikes. Starting blocks were a refinement not even contemplated. This was basic running but, Powderhall men proudly boast, their stars were men of genuine pace and ability. Ossie Oswald swears, for example, that Blyth's Albert Spence would have murdered Britain's Olympic sprinter of his day, Macdonald Bailey, a meeting once talked about for St. James's Park.

Milburn's potential was obvious and Les Common goes as far as to say: 'If Jackie had been an American, with specialised training over the years he would have made their Olympic team.'

CHAPTER FIVE

On Our Way

Season 1947-48 was a momentous season not only for Newcastle United but Wor Jackie himself. United were promoted to the First Division in front of record crowds and Jack not only got married but was switched to the centre-forward role which was to establish him as one of the all-time greats and see him finish the season as Newcastle's top scorer.

Jack recalled the excitement on Tyneside vividly when he told me: 'The whole place hummed. You couldn't shoe horn all the people into St. James's Park. There were 15,000 applications for the 1,500 season tickets and even we, the players, had to queue to get into the ground on match days. The size of the crowd meant that it sometimes took us three quarters of an hour to get up the bank and round to the players' entrance.

'Our average attendance that season was 56,351 which stood as a record anywhere in the country for years. Our supporters even flooded the club with clothing coupons to help kit out the side.'

The effect of the war wasn't quite over but United had thrown off the cloak of despondency and were about to take their first step into a golden era. The club had been marked by times when they touched greatness . . . the Edwardian team which challenged for the League and Cup every season at the beginning of the century, the Hughie Gallacher years which culminated in winning the First Division championship, and now the Wor Jackie years which were to bring the FA Cup to Tyneside three times in five seasons.

The match that virtually clinched promotion for Newcastle United in season 1947-48. Goalscorer Frank Houghton, who broke his arm, is helped up by trainer Norman Smith. In front of them is Tommy Walker with Jackie Milburn sitting on the ground.

Under a new manager, George Martin, 1947-48 was a season of high drama and a heart tugging finale. It was also a season of change — United sold star forwards Charlie Wayman, Len Shackleton, Roy Bentley and Stan Pearson, yet still achieved their goal. They were without the injured Duggie Wright throughout, and for long periods without Tommy Walker, who broke an arm in training, and Bobby Corbett, who had a cartilage operation.

But shrewd juggling brought success. Goalkeeper Jack Fairbrother arrived from Preston for £7,000; Norman Dodgin was promoted at wing-half; Frank Brennan's understudy Bob Fraser was used in several positions; full-backs Bobby Cowell and Benny Craig emerged; and Milburn was converted to centre-forward.

The date of that last, significant throw of the dice is marked in the annals of Newcastle United: October 18, 1947.

'It all came about because Charlie Wayman, who had never really regained his appetite after his semi-final axeing, suddenly signed for Southampton,' said Milburn. 'We had a lot of top class players in those days and one day Charlie walked in to find all the pegs in the dressing-room taken. "Bloody hell," he said. "I can't even get a peg now. I'm off" and he was, too, for £10,000.

'Charlie had been a natural goalscorer. He never lost the urge and would punch the sky in delight if he scored even in five-a-side training games. He was Johnny on the Spot, invaluable to wingers like me.

'His understudy George Stobbart was injured at the time and when George Martin, Stan Seymour, Joe Harvey, trainer Norman Smith and myself were sitting around talking, conversation got round to Wayman's successor. 'Jack's the man,' declared Martin.

'Naw, keep him at inside-left or on the wing,' said Norman Smith shaking his head. 'Aye, he's not good enough in the air for a centre forward,' agreed Seymour. I hurriedly agreed, insisting I was happy where I was. The thought of leading the line held no appeal to me but Martin refused to give in to such mass opposition. "You're wrong, all of you," he insisted with conviction. "I'll tell you something. Not only will Jackie make a centre forward but he'll get a cap into the bargain."

'For two nights before the game at Gigg Lane I never slept a wink but Lady Luck — and Shack — were to smile on me. Len told me in the dressing-room "Don't worry, Jackie, I'll look after you" and he did.

'Within five minutes the Bury goalkeeper George Bradshaw broke his leg and their whole team had to be shuffled with Harry Catterick going in goal. It meant I had a lot more room in which to work and against 10 men I managed to score three goals. The first was a fluke, the ball bobbling between my legs, and I went on to head another. Shack ran 50 yards to chortle "See what centre-forward's done for you — you're heading 'em in now!" '

United won 5-3 and Wor Jackie insisted that Shack nursed him through those early games as a No. 9. His love of the Yorkshireman with a splash of genius was total. Trevor Ford, a Welsh international centre-forward, was later to complain that he could never read Shack at Sunderland but Milburn had no such problems.

'I simply learned to expect the unexpected,' said Jack. 'If Shack

Somewhere in the jumble of arms and legs is Frank Houghton, the unlikely goalscoring hero against Sheffield Wednesday.

went one way I went the other — and, sure enough, the ball would arrive.'

Jack cited a game against Cardiff City at St. James's just after his conversion as a typical example of Len at his most lethal.

'After I scored in only six seconds we played some great stuff with Shackleton and Pearson mesmerising the crowd and the Cardiff defenders. Towards the end of the game they passed and re-passed the ball to each other for about five minutes with no one able to get anywhere near them. Finally Shack, arms akimbo and his foot on the ball, held three defenders transfixed before suddenly bursting past them like a greyhound from the traps to crash a shot against the Cardiff crossbar.'

The star forwards were to abandon United, however. Bentley left in the January of 1948 for Chelsea and an England career and the following month Pearson returned to his native Scotland to join Aberdeen and Shackleton made the short trip to neighbours Sunderland.

Shack's transfer, however, was the one with a touch of drama. Colonel Joe Prior (Sunderland), Norman Banks (Bolton Wanderers) and George Kay (Liverpool) were gathered for the final round of talks and each was asked to place his offer in a sealed envelope and return it to Newcastle's chairman George Rutherford. The astute Colonel Prior added £50 to the Sunderland bid and so Shack went off to Roker Park for £20,050, which was a record fee at the time.

If United were going through a period of change, then so was Jackie — and not just from the wing to centre-forward. On February 16, 1948 he got married only two months after meeting Laura on a training trip to Letchworth.

'I was sitting down to breakfast with Jack Fairbrother when I saw this girl. She was a member of the staff and I turned to Jack and said "I'm going to marry her." Honest. I don't know what it was but I knew straight away. It took me three days to pluck up courage to ask her out, mind you, and the first thing I did was to buy her a little silver dog from a jeweller's shop. It was her birthday, I think.

'We went to the pictures to see Greer Garson and Walter Pidgeon in *Mrs Miniver*. The training was only for a week so a couple of days later I was on my way back to Ashington leaving Laura behind. I rang her every day and persuaded her to come up and stay for a few weeks with my mam. Everybody liked her straight away and there was no sense in waiting so we set the date for Willesden Green registry office near where Laura was living. We didn't have a penny but I never was one to worry about tomorrow.

'I can remember Laura's dress. It was blue and cost me £3 17s 6d wholesale and she looked a treat. We got married on a Monday and had a small reception at her dad's house. Laura and I had two days in Folkestone afterwards but then I had to get back to Tyneside as we had a match against Coventry.

'I had to borrow £300 off my benefit to get married and set up home. Everything we had was second hand — there was still ration books and all that. We went round all the salerooms but I wouldn't buy anything on tick.

'I was still working as a fitter down the pit, I earned less than £3

Jackie and Laura pictured on their wedding day on February 16, 1948.

a week at the colliery and my football wage was £10 a week in winter and £7 in summer. Len Shackleton had just been transferred and we had to hang on for him to get out of his club house. Even though he was a good mate I was desperate for him to move.'

Laura, a Scots girl who had moved south with her family, knew nothing of Newcastle United and didn't know who Jackie was when they first met.

'I was only 20 and working in the hotel to save up enough money to go and live with my sister in Canada. But I never got to go. Jack was a real heart-throb in his young days. Very shy, though. I think people must have thought him a grumpy so-and-so he was so quiet. But in one week he got over 2,000 letters from fans. I can always remember we'd been to a dance of some kind and I'd met this young girl there. The next week Jack got a letter from this girl saying she'd met me and I was very nice and all that but if he ever got tired of me then she was available. I was hopping mad.'

United won promotion on the back of an impeccable home record which saw them win 18 times at St. James's Park. The climax was breathtaking like a Hollywood film script with a bit part actor taking over the John Wayne role.

One week in April virtually guaranteed promotion. Fulham were dispatched in midweek 1-0 in front of 54,061 through a Stobbart penalty and by the time the Saturday came 66,483 disciples had descended on St. James's Park with excitement at fever pitch. United were second in the table and their opponents, Sheffield Wednesday, third two points behind.

Newcastle were on song having won 10 games in succession at Gallowgate and not conceded a solitary goal at home for three months. But within 10 minutes, with the kids still being passed over the heads of the fans to sit down at the front, Wednesday were ahead. Benny Craig handled on the line and Whitcomb silenced the huge crowd by tucking away the penalty.

George Stobbart equalised during a rare spell of United pressure and then, shortly after the start of the second-half, skipper Joe Harvey rose to head one of his rare goals from a Tommy Walker corner. Relief poured from the terraces . . . surely now United were safe. But, no. Nine minutes from time courageous Wednesday levelled it at 2-2 with Marriott scoring and thousands of Geordies were biting their nails again.

With time running out United needed a hero. And they found one — but it wasn't the galloping Milburn, nor Walker, nor any of the stars. It was Frank Houghton, a wing-half from Ballymena but playing on the wing.

In the 87th minute Houghton nosed United in front again, his bravery seeing him clash with a defender and needing treatment. But he wasn't done, not by a long chalk. Two minutes later another valiant charge for the ball saw him force it home as he collided with the goalpost, breaking his arm and badly gashing his leg.

When Stockton referee Trenholm blew the final whistle the

Newcastle United players before the Probables v Possibles practice match at St. James's Park in 1949. Back row (left to right): manager George Martin, Milburn, Fairbrother, G. Robledo, Walker, Garbutt, Mitchell, Brennan, trainer Norman Smith. Centre row: Dodgin, Lowrie, Graham, Craig, Graver, Harvey, Fraser, Batty. Front row: Scott, Houghton, Thompson, Stobbart, Stephenson, Ted Robledo, Corbett.

noise was deafening. Manager George Martin stood at the mouth of the tunnel, both arms raised in triumph. United had blasted the door to the First Division open and a 1-1 draw at Spurs the following week confirmed the inevitable. Newcastle were up behind Birmingham City with Wednesday unluckily in third place.

Martin was to leave before the Cup exploits but Milburn, who owed him so much, maintained: 'He was a very likeable man whose main concern was the welfare of his players. He was always ready to help us get over any little financial worries. He would listen attentively if we reported a crack in the kitchen sink or in the ceiling, and would get it repaired on the double. If George overheard me mention that Laura was ill he would ring her up to ask how she was getting on. Attention to detail was his forte. He worked on the assumption that if you got the little things right then the big things would fall into place.'

The chopping and changing of United's promotion side was shown by the fact that only Brennan (42 appearances), Milburn (39) and Harvey (37) played more than 26 games each in the whole campaign. Jack's move to centre-forward had paid off handsomely — he was top scorer by a mile netting 20 goals out of United's 72 with Stobbart next on nine and the departed Shackleton on seven.

Jackie may have talked of Lady Luck, may have generously given credit to Shack, may have looked to praise Martin's foresight but to do so overlooks one vital ingredient . . . his own ABILITY. Milburn oozed that . . . lung bursting pace and a clout into the net's far corner. In heavy boots with a laced football, his power and grace were a sight to behold.

In those developing years Jackie listened intently to the advice of Hughie Gallacher, a genius of a player who tragically ended up committing suicide.

Gallacher was born in Bellshill, a typical Lanarkshire industrial community, and grew up with another soccer immortal Alex James. Gallacher's was certainly a troubled character, his brilliant career dogged by controversy and misfortune. But at Newcastle he was revered, scoring no fewer than 36 League goals when United won the First Division championship in 1927 and attracting a mammoth crowd of 68,586 when he came 'back home' with Chelsea three years later. Both stand to this very day as club records.

He loved Tyneside and came back here to live out his years until, in June of 1957, he walked in front of a train as it thundered over a crossing in Gateshead. Life had only been tolerable when he was playing football.

'We all owed our heritage to wee Hughie,' maintained Milburn. 'He began all the hero worship and the affinity with the No. 9 shirt at St. James's Park. When I was lucky enough to wear it he would wait for me on match days outside the main entrance, always at the same time in the same place, ten yards from the door. "Hi, Jackie, you're doing fine," he would say, "but I've got a little tip for you . . .", then he would mention something he had spotted in my play the previous game. "You're standing with your back to the centre-half and your team-mates don't know how to play the ball up to you. Why don't you half turn to give them a clue which side you want it and then run. They'll never catch you."

'Throughout my playing days I always listened intently to any advice the big names had to give. To me their words were worth a million from any coach. I once played with the great Hughie in a charity match when he was aged 52. He took a cross from the wing, jammed it against the goalpost with his head, and dropped it over the line. Who else could have done a thing like that?'

'I literally wept the day I learned he had walked onto the railway crossing and put his neck on the line to finish it all. How a man so loved and so idolised could feel so alone I'll never know.'

United took to the First Division in season 1948-49 like ducks to water. The crowds flocked in and, after a long spell in second place which was held until two matches from the end, they finished a most creditable fourth with Milburn top scoring on 19 goals, an incredible 13 more than nearest rival George Robledo who had joined the club in the January.

Then it was off on the *Queen Mary* to Canada on tour . . . after a row over their quarters which emphasised that, while Newcastle's players produced the goods, they expected first class treatment in return. When they boarded the ship at Southampton they discovered they had been put in the tourist class while Scotland's international squad were travelling first class. The senior players were annoyed and an emergency meeting was called. Eventually it was decided to send a deputation to the directors with an ultimatum: 'Better accommodation or we don't play in Canada.' Skipper Joe Harvey, always the team spokesman, saw Stan Seymour and the outcome was an instruction to remove their gear to the posh upper decks.

A minor squabble over — and to be fair United's board usually did things in style — and United coasted through their 10-match programme winning every game with displays of exhibition football. The goals poured from a tap never turned off with Wor Jackie the master marksman . . . four against Ontario All Stars in an 8-2 win, another six as Alberta All Stars were hammered 16-2, four more against Washington State helping to bring an 11-1 victory, five out of eight against Vancouver All Stars, and a hat-trick in a 4-0 demolition of Swedish side Kamaterna in Toronto.

The opposition may have regularly carried the misguided title of 'all stars' but in reality there was only one true star. Milburn, who scored in every match, totted up no fewer than 31 goals in 10 tour matches. An international had truly arrived.

CHAPTER SIX

Playing for England

English soccer just after the Second World War was packed with charismatic names . . . there was Frank Swift, the huge goalkeeper with bucket hands; Neil Franklin, a centre-half of finesse and the blond Billy Wright; Manchester United's wing-half Henry Cockburn; and two wingers of legendary prowess, Stanley Matthews and Tom Finney. Were there ever better men?

And, barring Jackie's way to the No. 9 shirt was one Tommy Lawton. Tall and slightly hunched with Brylcreemed hair parted at the centre, Lawton was a sharpshooter with a prodigious leap. He was a true marksman, England's champion scorer from those lethal Matthews' crosses.

But all sporting heroes, however great, must eventually bow the knee to the passing of time and England were beginning to think of Lawton's successor. The gaze turned north to Newcastle and Jackie Milburn.

The trial horse was always the inter-league games and so it came to pass that when the Football League side was named to play the Irish League in September of 1948 J.E.T. Milburn was at No. 9.

As in all good fairytales Jackie had always been one to make an auspicious start. Hadn't he scored six goals in the second-half of his trial game, a goal on his home debut, and a hat-trick in his first ever match as a centre-forward? That pattern was not to change.

Milburn duly scored three against the Irish League though, modest to a fault, he gave the bulk of the credit to his old sparring partner Len Shackleton who was playing at inside-left.

Milburn in the white shirt of England rounds the goalkeeper.

'Early in the game Shack dribbled through the Irish defence, rounded the keeper, and had the easiest task in the world to tap the ball into the empty net. Instead he pushed it back for me to hit first time into the roof of the goal. "A nice start for you", he smiled on our way back to the centre circle.'

The first step taken, Milburn was quickly drafted into the full England squad to play Denmark in Copenhagen shortly afterwards, though it was to be a gentle introduction with no place in the actual team. That still belonged to Lawton.

Such was the modest lifestyle of even the great footballers of that austere time that Jackie had never been in an aeroplane before. Billy Wright, sensing his nervousness, sat next to him during the flight to help ease away the fears.

England drew a disappointing game 0-0 and the lack of goals was enough to finally open the door to the pit lad from Ashington. On October 19 Milburn became the first Newcastle player since Duggie Wright in 1939 to wear the white shirt of England — a fact he read in the stop press of the *Evening Chronicle*.

The game was against Ireland at Windsor Park and it's worth recalling the two teams for a match which was to be a landmark for a player United fans now accepted as Wor Jackie.

England: Swift (Manchester City); Scott (Arsenal), Howe (Derby); Wright (Wolves), Franklin (Stoke), Cockburn (Manchester United); Matthews (Blackpool), Mortensen (Blackpool), Milburn (Newcastle), Pearson (Manchester United), Finney (Preston).

Northern Ireland: Smythe (Distillery); Carey (Manchester United), Martin (Aston Villa); Walsh W (Manchester City), Vernon (West Brom), Farrell (Everton); O'Driscoll (Swansea), McAlinden (Portsmouth), Walsh (West Brom), Tully (Glasgow Celtic), Eglinton (Everton).

It was Wright's first game as England skipper but the pressure was on the only new cap, Milburn, who was attempting to replace the great Tommy Lawton.

'The team was packed with big names and every one of them came across in the dressing-room to have a few words of encouragement — all, that is, except the greatest of them all, Stanley Matthews. He never looked my way and I felt uneasy but, just before the kick-off, he shuffled across. "I didn't say much in there," he said, "because it's out here that matters. Just get across to the far post when I get the ball and you'll be okay. Sometimes it'll hang when I cross it so give it time."

'I duly noted the advice and it worked a treat. The first time Matthews got away down the right I made for the back post, positioning myself some 10 yards out.

'Sure enough, the cross came high and deep. Two defenders jumped for the ball in front of me but I waited a split second before I took off. The cross hung and they were on their way down as I was on my way up which gave me that little bit extra

Wor Jackie splits the defence to get in a header.

height advantage and my header whipped into the net sweet as you like. I scored on my England debut because I listened to Stanley Matthews and we went on to win 6-2.'

The Maestro had scored the first goal, from a Milburn pass, while Stan Mortensen got a hat-trick and Stan Pearson the other. Morty had been a player who had transfixed the young Milburn when he was a ball boy at Portland Park and Stan guested for Ashington.

Jackie, always a touch superstitious, had been given a little ebony elephant Laura always carried in her handbag as a good luck charm and he carried it in the pocket of his shorts.

'As I ran back after my goal I tapped my pocket. The little elephant had done a good job.'

The Matthews v Finney debate — you know, who was the greater player? — not only raged when they were both at their height but goes on unabated today amongst the older generation who remember what they fondly call 'the good old days.' In fact they were to a large degree very different players . . . Matthews, unlike so many wingers, didn't like the ball played in front of him but to his feet. He would reduce the game to a walk or slow shuffle, mesmerising the full-back and then, whoosh, he was away to the bye-line and the cross was in. He played for Stoke City at the age of 50 years and five days, a man who unquestionably knew how to look after himself. A national institution.

If Matthews was the hypnotist, then Finney was as quick as a bullet in flight with a goalscoring hunger. Stan scored a mere three times for England after the war while Finney, known as the Preston plumber, claimed 30 goals. He could play on either wing or at centre-forward.

For Wor Jackie to play between two such immortals in the white shirt of England on his debut was a moment of sheer joy.

It was funny that Milburn should replace a master header in Lawton because he was never known for his prowess in the air. Sure, he had scored many a goal with his head in the pit yard but once he pulled on the striped shirt of Newcastle that ability seemed to leave him.

'My heading was something of a joke amongst the Newcastle players but in reality I could head as well as the next fella as long as I was on my own. Throughout my playing career I suffered from fibrositis and was terrified of jumping with anyone in case my neck stuck. If it did I was unable to do anything except lie in bed and Laura even had to clean my teeth.

'The club spent a fortune on trying to help me and I hate to think how many goals I might have had had I been fully fit. I reckon fibrositis cost me more than 50 goals over my career as a whole but all the same I didn't do so badly. I scored with my head on my England debut, scored in an F.A. Cup Final and got two headers in my only England hat-trick against Wales and my bogeyman Tommy Jones of Everton.'

When Wor Jackie wore his country's colours with pride every household didn't possess the now mandatary television set with instant replays of his spectacular goals. Football was just stepping into a new age — the football pools, a social phenomenon of the 1930s, would only see the Football Association at last accept their inevitability and benefit financially in the 50s. TV and its instant livingroom stars largely lay ahead of Jackie's time . . . hence, perhaps, the huge crowds needing to see things for themselves.

England line up for the camera with Milburn on the right in the back row.

Radio, or the wireless as it was known to us of the working classes, was the dream maker, descriptive words of wondrous deeds on far off battlefields lifting the lives of those with mundane routines. Families, or at least the menfolk, would huddle round sets to listen to the voice of the likes of Raymond Glendenning bringing word pictures which would capture our imagination.

Otherwise it was the flickering newsreels at the cinema. Something which Bobby Charlton, then a wide eyed youngster, recalls from his childhood in Ashington.

'My brother Jack and I went to the pictures to see the newsreel of Jackie's first international against Ireland. We were late and had to sit through Moira Shearer in *The Red Shoes* until it was repeated.

'Our Jack and I as kids used to sit on the track at St. James's Park and watch Jackie play. He was very fast and his ball control at speed was as good as anyone I've seen. He'd run at defenders to make them commit themselves and I particularly remember him repeatedly embarrassing the most feared centre-half in the League, Jack Froggatt of Portsmouth.'

His international debut in Ireland led directly to the unthinkable . . . Jackie Milburn asking for a transfer. It was a moment of weakness so many young players have fallen for since, the first time they mix with international players from other clubs and hear of the money supposedly flying about.

Milburn honestly recalled: 'It was on the night boat from Belfast that the chat began. The wise boys got talking and, naturally I think, they whetted my appetite. As an England player they told me I could demand a good job outside of football if I was transferred to another club. And when I thought of my little house bought on HP and the struggle we were having I was extremely tempted. Laura hadn't been too well since she moved to the North East and I decided to make that my excuse.

'But United turned down my request out of hand and, to be truthful, I was delighted. I'd been daft to think of easy pickings but then the grass is always greener isn't it?

'United were always a clean club. There were no under the counter payments that went on elsewhere. The chairman George Rutherford would have no hanky panky. Whenever I joined up with England I would hear players from other clubs talking about 'programme money' and for a long time I wondered what on earth they were on about. Programme money, it turned out, was surplus cash raised by clubs on match days, probably through the sale of match programmes, and then shared out among the players. I often heard that expression — but never at Newcastle. There was nowt like that for us.'

The 1948-49 season brought Jackie further caps against Wales, Switzerland and Scotland. Though England defeated Wales 1-0 it wasn't a classical performance with an injury to right-back Laurie Scott, who was never to play another international, disrupting the team and taking Stan Mortensen from Milburn's side to play emergency right-half.

But at Highbury it was England and not the Swiss who played like clockwork. The team was greatly changed . . . out had gone Frank Swift, Stan Pearson and Tom Finney along with Scott, and debuts were handed to Alf Ramsey, embarking on an outstanding career, Spurs keeper Ted Ditchburn, little Johnny

England's stars again. Milburn is sitting between Tom Finney and skipper Billy Wright with the front row completed by South Shields-born Stan Mortensen and former United star Len Shackleton.

Hancocks of Wolves, Manchester United's Jack Rowley, and West Brom's Jack Haines.

That day England were touched by angels. Everything they tried came off and they powered their way to a convincing 6-0 victory. Haines, playing in his first and only international, made it personally memorable by scoring twice while two other debut boys, Hancocks (2) and Rowley, also got on the scoresheet. Oh, and so did Milburn!

Perhaps few realised at the time but it was to mark the beginning of a distinguished England career for Ramsey, who went on to be knighted when, as manager, he was the brains behind England winning the World Cup in 1966. Ramsey, then of Southampton, was a right-back with the distribution of an inside-forward and he showed his maturity by playing the ball to the wizard of the dribble, Stanley Matthews, and then yelling: 'Hold it!'

'We'd never heard a senior player do that to Stan never mind a newcomer,' said Jackie. 'We were all amazed at his confidence.'

Milburn, the man for the Command Performance, was to make Wembley his stage with United in the future, but his first appearance on the hallowed turf was in the big international of the season against Scotland. And it wasn't to be a particularly happy one.

England were bursting with big names . . . Swift was back, there was skipper Billy Wright and Neil Franklin, and Milburn's front line partners were Stan Matthews, Stan Mortensen, Stan Pearson and Tom Finney. The Scots, too, had men of stature. There was the giant George Young of Glasgow Rangers, the flame haired Bobby Evans from Celtic, centre-half Willie Woodburn of Rangers, Derby's splendid inside-forward Bill Steel and Hibernian leader Laurie Reilly. Plus Morton's renowned goalkeeper Jimmy Cowan, who was to break England's heart on an afternoon of undiluted pleasure for the Tartan hordes.

England began like an express train, repeatedly cutting huge swathes through the Scottish defence. It was one way traffic but Cowan was in majestic form, stopping shots he had no right to lay a finger on.

After the match Milburn lamented: 'When Jimmy saved at least three shots of mine which I imagined would go past him I suspected he knew precisely where the ball was going to go even before it left my foot. As is often the case when a team dominates a match and doesn't score we were hit badly on the break. Jimmy Mason, Bill Steel and Laurie Reilly all struck splendid goals to give the Scots a three-goal lead and send their followers into raptures.

'I managed to pull a goal back when I turned in a shot by Morty which was going wide but we lost 3-1 and it was a long trek back to the dressing-room. I felt dreadful even though I'd scored in my first game at Wembley but a lot of Wembley joy lay ahead for me with United.

'Stan Seymour, who was at the match, reckoned I'd not got the support I needed, which might have been true, but it didn't wash away the feeling of disappointment.'

CHAPTER SEVEN

The World Cup

During 1949 the Football Association came to a momentous decision — for the first time England would take part in the World Cup, or the Jules Rimet Trophy as it was then known, if they qualified. The idea had been born in France and came to fruition in 1930 when the first tournament was staged in Uruguay. Only four European countries agreed to take part and with Britain having withdrawn from FIFA we ignored the early tournaments.

But the four British Associations had returned to FIFA in 1946 and the World Cup Committee had indulgently designated the British Championship a qualifying zone for the 1950 finals to be held in Brazil. Two teams were to go through but Scotland rewarded the committee's courtesy by sullenly and indefensibly announcing that unless they won the British title they would not compete.

It made the 1949-50 international season one of extra significance and Milburn, as England's elected leader of their forward line, looked longingly towards Rio and the newly planned 200,000 capacity Maracana Stadium by the banks of the Maracana River.

Wor Jackie and England couldn't have got off to a better start. The Welsh, backed by the vocal choir echoing 'Land of my Fathers' to every corner of Ninian Park, were comprehensively beaten 4-1 with the pace and opportunism of United's top star producing a magnificent hat-trick.

Finney remembers the match with clarity. 'Before the kick-off Jackie said to me: "I'm facing Jones again today. I never get owt out of him." I replied: "Don't be daft. Forget all about him. Go out and get a hat-trick." And Milburn did just that.'

But his joy was to be short-lived with Jackie, at the very height of his England form, breaking his right wrist, an injury which had long-lasting effects and kept him out of the rest of the British championships. England duly qualified for Rio, beating Scotland with a goal from former United star Roy Bentley, and the Scots, licking their wounds, withdrew from the World Cup.

Had Jack's chances of going to South America disappeared? He thought they probably had but when England's party to visit Portugal and Belgium in a pre-Rio tour was announced he'd been given an 11th-hour reprieve.

The Portuguese National Stadium, hewn out of a valley near Estoril at a cost of £350,000, was breathtaking and England duly obliged with a 5-3 victory. Milburn, the marauding centre-forward, was drafted into the outside-right position so long dominated by Matthews and Finney, and though he didn't score (Finney got four including two penalties) he knew in his heart of hearts that he had done himself justice.

Belgium were next at the Heysel Stadium, the venue many years later for tragedy when Liverpool played a European cup-tie and thirty-nine fans were killed. Milburn again struck a seam of gold and was playing out of his skin when, sprinting down the wing, his right foot turned over in a small hole and down he went to be carried off by ambulance men.

'I was convinced I'd broken my ankle and it was bye, bye Rio but 15 minutes later I could sprint with no pain. The only trouble was that, for the first time in international football, England had used a substitute, sending on Jimmy Mullen of Wolves, and I couldn't return to the field of play. I sat squirming as England fought back from a goal down to win 4-1 with Bentley carving 'em up.'

Milburn needn't have worried. Within a week of arriving home the England party for their first ever World Cup was announced and he was in.

The pit yacker from Ashington was to embark on one of the greatest adventures he could ever have dreamed of during those kickabouts in the cobbled back lanes with his schoolmates.

Milburn's own signed picture of England on the steps of their hotel in Estoril, near Lisbon in 1950. He is in the front row between Wilf Mannion and Tom Finney.

England, the home of football, were hailed as 'Soccer's Kings' when they touched down in Rio after the 6,000 mile trip had taken an exhausting 31 hours. The excitement and the interest were immense; England had been installed as one of the favourites for the tournament and everyone wanted to know about the giants from the other side of the world.

England's party were housed at the Luxor Hotel, 20 yards from the sun-kissed beach of Copacabana and for Milburn, sharing a room with fellow Geordie Stan Mortensen, it was a time of wide-eyed wonderment.

'Everything was so different from Ashington. Our hotel room cost £10 a night, without breakfast, and from our balcony you could watch magnificent girls walking past as though they were straight out of a fashion book. Then, just to jar you, a poor and dejected cripple would hobble after them.

'But it was a beautiful scene by night with the twinkling lights playing on Copacabana Beach and the huge floodlit figure of Christ poised on the top of Mount Corovado with outstretched hands reaching over the whole city. The main highway was dead straight and the high-powered American Cadillacs raced along the stretch as though it was Brooklands.

'Literally dozens of football pitches were laid out on the sands. Here, beneath floodlights, matches were played with young boys hoping to attract the attention of the big South American clubs. The negroes had outstanding ball control and whenever they knew we were watching they went out of their way to put on an exhibition.'

England, under their first-ever full-time manager in Walter Winterbottom, were to kick off against Chile who were to include Milburn's great goalscoring pal George Robledo. Perhaps not unnaturally they decided to stick with the side which had seen off Belgium after Jackie's early departure and that meant Finney on the right, Mullen on the left, and Bentley at centre-forward. There was no place for Matthews, who had been playing for England since 1934 and was now 35 years old. He hadn't played in the internationals during the 1949-50 season and had been sent off in an F.A. party to tour Canada and New York.

The Brazilians had been caught out by the suddenness of the World Cup. They had lavished £3,000,000 on the Maracana Stadium but when England turned up to watch the opening match between the home country and Mexico 7,000 workmen were still tearing down the scaffolding!

'We had to clamber over barbed wire, wade through builders' materials and even avoid a burst pipe gushing water. The smell of drying cement was everywhere but, once in the stadium, the scene was unbelievable. As Brazil ran out hundreds of firecrackers lit up the sky and 5,000 pigeons were released. Before Brazil kicked off there was a 21 gun salute. Everyone went crazy — and it lasted for the full 90 minutes.'

Brazil won 4-0 and the following day, a Sunday, England beat Chile 2-0 without hitting anything like sound form. Stan Mortensen and Wilf Mannion were the executioners and a thunderstorm a few hours before the kick-off meant there was no need for the oxygen which had been placed in the England dressing-room to be used at half-time.

Robledo was the only professional in the Chile side. The rest

Milburn in action for England against France at Highbury in 1951.

were engineers, bootmakers, accountants and grocers who got £14 a month to play part-time.

But Alf Ramsey revealed: 'Robledo was outstanding. Throughout the match he distributed the ball extremely well and when a free-kick was awarded against us and the English defence lined up, George still contrived to find a hole through which to crash a terrific drive which nearly bent an upright before rebounding for me to hook the ball away. "Don't forget we're your pals, George," I told him as the ball hit touch.'

Next were the United States . . . a doddle, a stroll before the bigger games ahead. The Yanks, hardly one of soccer's greater nations, were a hotch potch of a side. They were captained from right-half by Eddie McIlvenny, a Scot who only 18 months earlier had been given a free transfer by Third Division Wrexham and emigrated. Maca, the left-back, was a Belgian and centre-forward Larry Gaetjens from Haiti. Their manager, Bill Jeffrey, was another Scot who had gone west 30 years earlier and combined coaching with teaching in a machine shop.

They were hardly likely to test the cream of English football, especially as just over a week earlier they had lost to a much less talented F.A. XI in New York. Okay, in their opening match the United States had courageously led Spain until the final 10 minutes before surrendering 3-1, but England — that would be different.

The match was to be played at Belo Horizonte — the beautiful horizon — which lay 280 miles inland and the only question to be answered was whether England played their 'reserve' side which hadn't had a run-out in Rio or kept the same team which beat Chile to give them extra match practice.

Milburn, it was suggested, could at least expect to come in but the injury jinx which had cruelly struck him down against Wales and Belgium again surfaced to scupper all his hopes. Jumping to head a cross from Matthews in training, he landed heavily on the hard ground jarring every bone in his body.

'The outcome was a severe attack of fibrositis and for four days my neck was swathed in bandages. I was in great pain and had no chance of playing against the United States.'

It may have appeared that fate had dealt him a bad hand again, but as things turned out, it was to be a blessing in disguise. For ahead lay the blackest day in the history of English football. The biggest humiliation we had ever experienced. Not that the Yanks felt they were on the verge of history. Their manager, Bill Jeffrey, stated publicly that they had no chance and several of his players stayed up into the small hours the night before.

Sure, the little stadium, with its bumpy surface and inadequate changing facilities, was primitive but otherwise England seemed in clover. The mountain air, by contrast with that of Rio, was invigorating and the party had stayed happily as guests of the Morro Velho gold mine, English owned and employing 2,000 British workers. But what was to come was horrific, a shattering 1-0 defeat which was to resound round the world.

Perhaps it's best to recall the sensation through the eyes of three England players present — Milburn, Matthews and Ramsey.

Milburn, who sat in the stand next to Matthews and Eddie Bailey, maintained: 'We set a fast pace. Wilf Mannion was on song and the Americans were dazzled but goals just wouldn't come.

George Robledo, who played against England in the 1950 World Cup finals in Brazil, pictured in Chile's strip with a young fan.

Our players tried hard, maybe a little too hard, and just before half-time the impossible happened. The United States scored a freak goal and we went into the dressing-room one down.

'I remember turning to Willie Watson and saying: "It shouldn't be difficult for us to coast this match." We should have, too, even though the Americans played well with Ed Souzar, a balding inside-left, outstanding. Their keeper made saves no keeper has a right to make. Sometimes he stopped shots without knowing too much about them. Even Alf Ramsey sauntered upfield for a pot shot and we should have scored ten.'

Matthews added: 'The Americans were the favourites of the crowd right from the start. I suppose it was because they were the underdogs. As it was, handicapped by the small pitch and not finding true form, we found ourselves behind five minutes before half-time when Gaetjens headed in a centre from the right wing. England were disturbed but I hoped the goal would act as a pin prick and get the boys going but it was not to be.'

Ramsey, who actually suffered the humiliation of playing, declared: 'We had a year's bad luck in 90 minutes. Shots which appeared certain to score missed by the width of a coat of paint. And then, tragedy of tragedies. The American right winger swung over a hard cross and Bert Williams moved to take it. At that moment Gaetjens ducked to avoid the ball but by a million to one freak the ball touched the top of his head and was deflected into the net. To say that we were stunned is an understatement. If there had been an earthquake at Belo we couldn't have received a greater shock.

'In the second-half we resumed as we had left off by giving the American defence a real hammering. Once Stan Mortensen whipped in a fine shot which folk behind the goal declared was yards over the line but before the referee could get up with the play the ball was pushed back and he waved play on. On another occasion when Morty just had the keeper to beat a defender hauled him to the ground with as fine a rugby tackle as you'd ever see at Twickenham.

'Five minutes from time the crowd brought out their handkerchiefs and began waving farewell to England from the World Cup. It was a harrowing experience.'

Ramsey went on: 'Just how McIlvenny and one or two others qualified for the United States was a poser which FIFA officials later had to sit down and discuss. A footballer could only play in the World Cup for the country where he was born so England, if they had felt that way, could have lodged a protest against America for calling on players such as McIlvenny.'

That, of course, would have smacked of sour grapes. England had no complaints beforehand about facing a Third Division free transfer man and ought to have been capable of winning on merit, not by default.

England, tails between their legs, went back to Rio to try their last throw of the dice against Spain. Reports had told them that the Spanish backs played square and were vulnerable to the through pass. Milburn, the perfect forward to exploit this with his marvellous sprinting, was preferred to Bentley. Matthews was brought in on the right and Finney moved to the left. Bill Eckersley, in at left-back for Jack Aston, and Eddie Bailey, preferred to Wilf Mannion at inside-left, were playing in their first full international.

After 14 minutes Wor Jackie headed Finney's centre past the otherwise unbeatable Spanish reserve goalkeeper Ramallets, but the goal was disallowed for offside by Italian referee Signor Galeati. Newsreel photographs would show a Spanish defender playing Milburn onside but as it was Zarra headed in Basora's centre for the winner five minutes after half-time.

'When Finney pulled a centre back to me I couldn't possibly have been offside as a photograph later showed. But then the referee had a bad 'un letting the Spaniards get away with common assault on some of our players. They resorted to shirt pulling, body checking and tripping and thought nothing of intercepting passes with their hands.'

Twice Matthews was pulled back by his shirt after weaving past a defender and both Milburn and Mortensen were tripped inside the box. And, to cap it all, when Bailey, with a delightful feint, opened up the Spanish defence with a pass through the middle for Morty, a defender went full length to catch the ball and got up laughing.

On Milburn's 'goal' Ramsey insisted: 'It was perfectly all right. The referee made the mistake of not watching the position Jackie had occupied when the ball was kicked and film later proved we'd been robbed of a perfectly good goal splendidly taken by Milburn.'

Good goal or not England were out of the World Cup on their first appearance. It had been a new experience in a new world but the harrowing defeat by the United States was to hang over them like a big black cloud.

Back in 1950 there was no World Cup final as such. Instead there were final pool matches with Uruguay, claiming two victories and a draw, finishing on five points to lift the Jules Rimet Trophy ahead of hosts Brazil with a point less.

By now Jackie had eight England caps and was to go on to collect 13 in all, scoring ten goals. The following season at home, 1950-51, saw Milburn crack in four goals in three international appearances as he stayed at the very top . . . one goal in a 4-2 victory over Wales at nearby Roker Park in Sunderland, another at Wembley as a 1-0 half-time deficit was turned into a 2-1 win over Argentina, and two more as Portugal were sent packing 5-2 at Goodison Park.

However, the same season marked the England debut of a centre-forward who was to deprive him of many more caps in seasons to come: Bolton's Nat Lofthouse. If Milburn had heralded the end of a great leader in Tommy Lawton then Nat Lofthouse, who had attended the same school in Bolton as Lawton, was to make it extremely difficult for Jackie. Here were two men of a kind and only one could play regularly. Inspirational leaders both, but sadly of the same generation. If it was a flip of the coin it was Lofthouse who repeatedly got the nod, but then players of the outstanding pedigree of Matthews and Finney had felt the cold steel of the England selectors, so Wor Jackie wasn't alone.

One cap came in 1951-52 in a 2-2 draw with France at Highbury and then, belatedly, the final England honour on October 2, 1955 against Denmark in Copenhagen. Lofthouse led the line as usual with Milburn at outside-right. While old faces Wright and Finney remained there was a whole new generation of England players like full-backs Hall (Birmingham) and Byrne (Manchester United), wing-half McGarry of Wolves and inside-forward Revie from Manchester City. Jack signed off with a flourish, helping England to a 5-1 away win.

Milburn never knew the benefit of caps picked up on the cheap . . . two-minute appearances as a sub totting up a total to a false level. His were earned the hard way yet his final figures were impressive with his goals ratio good. They read:

Date	*Opposition*	*Result*	*Milburn goals*
9.10.48	Ireland	Won 6-2	1
10.11.48	Wales	Won 1-0	—
2.12.48	Switzerland	Won 6-0	1
9. 4.49	Scotland	Lost 3-1	1
15.10.49	Wales	Won 4-1	3
14. 5.50	Portugal	Won 5-3	—
18. 5.50	Belgium	Won 4-1	—
1950 World Cup	Spain	Lost 1-0	—
15.11.50	Wales	Won 4-2	1
9. 5.51	Argentina	Won 2-1	1
19. 5.51	Portugal	Won 5-2	2
3.10.51	France	Drew 2-2	—
2.10.55	Denmark	Won 5-1	—

Lawton described his England successor as 'like a streak of lightning with thunder in his boots' while United skipper Joe Harvey admitted: 'Jackie was unlucky to run into Lofthouse's era but England's loss was our gain.'

CHAPTER EIGHT

Glorious Wembley

The early fifties saw the shackles of war finally cast asunder and a bright new future drawn for Newcastle United. Thrice the mighty Magpies marched on Wembley and thrice they brought home the F.A. Cup. It was a time of jubilation and celebration and no one strode the glory trail with a more cavalier step than Jackie Milburn, the pit lad who wrote his name into the annals of Wembley history rubbing shoulders with Royalty and Prime Ministers. It was a time of triumph for the common man, a symbol that greatness can be achieved from even the humblest of beginnings.

Wor Jackie finally and deservedly wore the crown which was always destined for his head, scoring wondrous goals on a stage which befits a king. His was the name on the lips of a nation and never more so than in 1951, perhaps the finest of United's all-conquering Cup sides.

Milburn's display on the first of his Wembley visits was one for the connoisseur. Fifty-one was indeed a vintage year.

United's team was packed with great stars. In goal was Jack Fairbrother, a jovial, big-eyed goalkeeper who wore the white gloves of a policeman on point duty and worked his angles out to perfection. At full-back were Bobby Cowell and Bobby Corbett, two local lads with the bite of a beartrap. Right-half and skipper was Joe Harvey, the epitome of a driving force with a clenched fist to wave under the nose of any flagging player. Centre-half, the awesome Frank Brennan, who would roll up his sleeves, tell his

Newcastle United's Cup stars in old-fashioned track suits pictured in front of the team coach.

full-backs to 'piss off' and get on destroying his unlucky opponent. Left-half fell to Charlie Crowe, another of the early Stan Seymour local pick-ups during the war.

The forward line began with Tommy Walker, who could motor a bit; boasted tiny tot Ernie Taylor, creator surpreme at inside-right; Wor Jackie; Chilean goal ace George Robledo; and Bobby Mitchell, a left winger with twinkle toes who could have the crowd swaying with one movement of his hips.

Milburn called them The Best. And they were — with Jackie the shining star at the centre. There may have been Brennan, Harvey, Taylor and Mitch but Wor Jackie was the crowd's favourite son.

United may well have done the double of League and Cup, such was the balance, panache and ability of the side but, with no European Cup reward for the champions, the incentive was never quite there once the instant glamour of Wembley's great stage beckoned.

Milburn recognised the fact, telling me the players could see no further than the twin towers 'where the occasion and the stage were there to produce the performance rather than the chase for two points and perhaps a championship gifted because another side lost.'

Hard facts bear out the Milburn philosophy. United went unbeaten for 10 games from the opening fixture of the 1950-51 season to underline their potential, yet between the semi-final and final, with Wembley on their minds, they won but one of 11 games.

With manager George Martin now departed and Seymour pulling the strings United took to the Cup trail by beating Second Division Bury 4-1 at St. James's without big Brennan, a tonsillitis victim.

Brennan was an amazing character . . . a puny 2½lb baby who grew into a 6ft 3in, 14st centre-half who would scoff a dozen eggs and 10 rashers of bacon for breakfast. Hewn out of granite and deceptively quick for a big man, he was the complete stopper whose he-man antics forged a special affinity with the fans. Few centre-forwards fancied being cut down by the Scot who used to play for Father Dooley's team in Coatbridge. After Bury came a more testing challenge in the fourth round from Bolton Wanderers, a side which boasted amongst others a centre-forward of the Milburn mould in Nat Lofthouse. Without the combative Brennan United perhaps had cause to be a trifle apprehensive but his deputy Matt McNeil, another 6ft 3in tall Scot, played Lofthouse well and United came back from 2-1 down at the interval to win 4-2. Mitch had struck a goal in three minutes but it was Wor Jackie who was the hero, giving a taste of what was to come with two splendid second-half goals to the delight of 67,596 fans.

Stoke, never a match for United who had Brennan back, were dispatched 4-2 at the Victoria Ground with Milburn's great pal George Robledo scoring twice. George and his brother Ted were Chileans who had emigrated to England with their Yorkshire mother as tiny tots and joined United from Barnsley in a double deal worth £26,500. George was by far the greater star, an immensely strong goalscorer and perfect foil for Milburn.

As round six approached excitement in the North East reached fever pitch.

Sunderland were also going strong but instead of a Tyne-Wear derby which would have electrified the area United were drawn against Bristol Rovers, a side which cost a mere £350 to assemble.

Milburn, third from the right, cleverly turns a Tommy Walker corner into the Bury net on the way to the 1951 Cup final.

Like a lot of underdogs Rovers had their fleeting moment of glory, holding the Magpies to a draw at St. James's Park, but the replay saw Newcastle in no mood to prolong their headlines and they duly brought them to heel 3-1, Milburn scoring along with Taylor and Crowe.

That brought a semi-final clash with Wolves, 3-1 victors over Sunderland. At Hillsborough in Sheffield Newcastle did everything but score with the cat-like Bert Williams denying them all but a 0-0 draw. Four days later at Huddersfield Wolves took the lead, only this time even the brilliant Williams couldn't prevent Newcastle's march on Wembley. Two goals in the space of 40 seconds during the first-half sent the Magpies through to their eighth Cup final. On the half hour Taylor, an imp in football boots, evaded three tackles to set up Milburn and less than a minute later Jackie dispossessed centre-half Shorthouse to cross for Mitchell to score a crucial second.

Williams, an England regular, denied all the greats in a long and distinguished career but always maintained he couldn't 'read' Wor Jackie. His short back lift meant a keeper never knew when he was

Milburn scores against Wolves and England keeper Bert Williams in the 1951 semi-final replay at Huddersfield. Williams reckoned he could never read Wor Jackie with his short backlift and high follow through and this is a perfect example.

going to shoot but such was the power in his drive that his follow through would take his boot way above his head.

Brother-in-law Les Common had a premonition about United's glory run to Wembley.

'I was playing for Tow Law at the time but for some reason I always felt that United were going to win the Cup and consequently I took every Saturday off when there was a cup-tie. I don't know why I felt like that — sure, United were a fine side — but it was just a feeling. I never missed a solitary game home or away and I was sitting with the rest of Jackie's family in the stand for the final.'

Blackpool were to be United's opponents on the great day and every neutral in the land was behind them. Stanley Matthews had achieved everything there was to achieve in football bar one thing — a Cup winner's medal. This was to be his year. Only no one told Newcastle United.

Wor Jackie, he of the winged feet, had scored in every round on the way to Wembley and April 28 was to be his day rather than Matthews'.

Talking with him years later, when retirement had brought the contentment of a job well done, the excitement still came flooding back.

'That was the greatest side I was ever associated with. It was a dream to play with them, a privilege. We simply felt we couldn't be beaten if the prize was big enough. I lived by goals, they were my stock in trade, and my two in the '51 final were particularly

Wor Jackie scores the first of his two great goals against Blackpool in the 1951 final.

satisfying because they gave me the chance to display contrasting skills.

'The more famous of the two became known as the backheel goal. Tommy Walker pushed the ball to little Ernie Taylor and as he did I yelled: "Backheel it!" Ernie did but even so I was really too far over the ball. I struck it with all my might from 28 yards and it flew straight as an arrow into the back of the net. Had I been better positioned when I made contact it would probably have hit the crossbar.

'But for me the goal that mattered was the other one. This was a goal for the connoisseur, the one every centre-forward dreams of scoring. I remember starting my run from the halfway line, then running and running until I forced the goalkeeper, George Farm, to commit himself. Then all I had to do was tuck the ball home in the gap he had unwittingly opened up. I knew from the moment the ball left my foot that I'd scored and I turned away without even waiting to see the ball hit the back of the net.

'The trouble with a free run like that is that you can't believe what's happening. You keep seeing imaginary shadows chasing you and you're convinced you can feel the panting breath of half a dozen defenders down the back of your neck. That's why it means so much to score, so many things could go wrong.

'That was our first goal and as I returned to the halfway line Stan Mortensen shook me by the hand and said: "Jackie, if we have to lose I'm glad it's to a goal like that." We had that sort of camaraderie in those days.

'Actually, I should have become the first player ever to score a hat-trick in a Wembley Cup final because, before I got my two, I had the ball in the net chesting it down and sticking it between Farm's legs, but it was chalked off by referee Bill Ling. Hand ball, he said, but he was wrong — I never touched it.

'A lot of folk tried to say it was a one man show at Wembley, but it wasn't of course. How could it be? We had to keep Matthews quiet and I could hardly do that. No, that credit belongs to left-back Bobby Corbett and left-half Charlie Crowe. Our tactics were to have Crowe drop back to help shadow Matthews, snapping at his heels and never allowing him to settle on the ball and pick up the impetus of a run at his full-back. If you allowed him to do that you were dead.

'On the day Matthews never really got a kick and I was able to get the two goals which won us the Cup.'

Matthews, later to get that elusive winner's medal, saw United's victory thus: 'Five minutes after the interval Jackie Mudie pushed the ball through to me. I managed to beat Bobby Corbett and cut along the line. I spotted Morty making a typical dash down the middle and quickly cut the ball back. It was too fast for him, he raced back but stumbled and George Robledo fastened onto the ball and was away. George passed to Jackie Milburn who ran through, drew Farm, and scored.

'Five minutes later Milburn crashed in a dream goal from nearly 30 yards to make it 2-0 and seal our fate. He took a chance, it came off, and as a result the match will always be remembered as the Milburn final.'

Les Common, even allowing for family bias, was particularly enthralled by Wor Jackie's first.

'I've watched the film clip time and time again and, as the ball is played up to Jackie, you can see Blackpool's centre-half Eric Haywood looking appealingly for offside. Jack, just inside his own half, glanced across at the linesman, then stepped up a gear and was away past Haywood with the Blackpool full-backs caught square. It was a beautiful piece of sprinting.'

Yet before Milburn scored the greatest goals Wembley had seen he sat in the dressing-room at half-time smoking a fag! No fewer than nine of the team were smokers and Seymour, who believed

Blackpool keeper George Farm is beaten after Ernie Taylor's famous backheel.

in treating men as men, would dish out a packet of Player's cigarettes on the platform at the Central Station before all long train journeys to away matches. Jack was lucky — his mate George Robledo was a non-smoker and so he finished up with two packets.

United were to be back at Wembley the next year as the partnership between Milburn and Robledo became the most feared in the land. Jackie kicked off with a hat-trick on the opening day in a 6-0 demolition of Stoke and by the time April came round Robledo had plundered an incredible 39 goals and Milburn 28. They went together like fish and chips, no one could touch them.

But even in a small space of time great teams change. In the September of the new season Fairbrother broke his collarbone against Manchester United and never played football again. His place went to Ronnie Simpson, a spidery-legged keeper brought

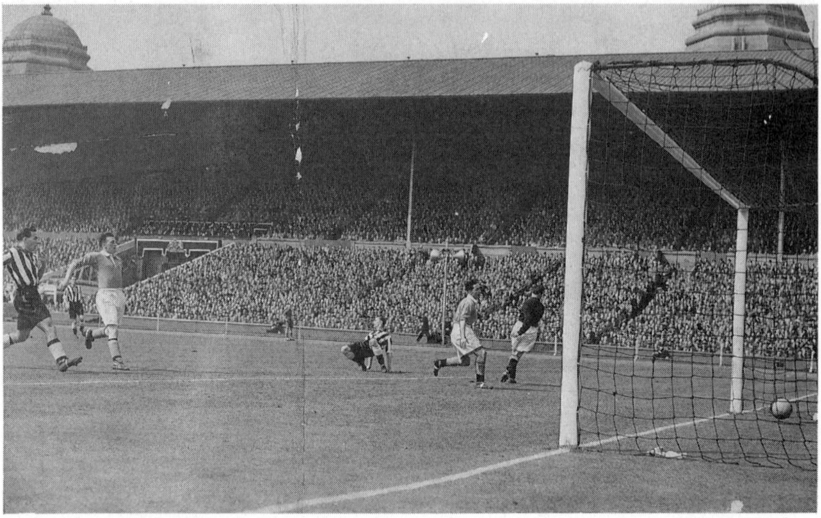

The Milburn goal which didn't count. He's pictured during a balancing act after slipping the ball through Farm's legs.

down from Third Lanark for £8,750, but in reality the writing had been on the wall for jovial Jack long before then.

While the champagne was still flowing in Newcastle's hotel after the first Cup win Fairbrother, now in his thirties, had overheard a director saying: 'It's the last time he plays for us — he's finished now.' It was loose talk, no doubt brought about by the effects of alcohol, but it hurt the big keeper who slipped away from the party, bags packed, to go home. Luckily, Joe Harvey and Bobby Mitchell gave chase and hauled him back to the celebrations from the platform of King's Cross Station.

Milburn's summing up of United's two Wembley keepers was precise: 'Fairbrother was the master of angles and consequently rarely had to throw himself around. The ball inevitably came to his chest. He practised to perfect his art and many's the time I acted as his stooge, the attacker shooting on the run. He would tie a rope to the goalpost and give me the other end. As I ran in to smack a shot at him the rope would indicate exactly where Jack should be standing to take the shot. We would work until the sweat was rolling down my face and Jack got his sums right.

'But I'll tell you something — Fairbrother was the only keeper I've known who I always felt would save any shot. And I played

Blackpool denied as Jack Fairbrother (in cap) palms the ball away watched by Frank Brennan (No. 5), Bobby Cowell and Blackpool's Stan Mortensen.

for England with the likes of Frank Swift, Ted Ditchburn and Bert Williams.

'Simpson was a goal-line keeper with spectacular lightning reflexes. He would stop as many shots with his feet as his hands.

The greatest team Jackie ever played in — Newcastle United's 1951 side. Back row (left to right): Bobby Cowell, Joe Harvey, Frank Brennan, Jack Fairbrother, Bobby Corbett, Charlie Crowe. Front row: Tommy Walker, Ernie Taylor, Jackie Milburn, George Robledo, Bobby Mitchell.

He had a habit of walking on the balls of his feet as though always ready to spring. The only thing which prevented Ronnie being an all-time great was his lack of inches which meant he never dominated the penalty area.'

Simpson himself paid tribute to Fairbrother, who helped him greatly when he first arrived at St. James's Park.

'I don't think I've ever met a goalkeeper quite like Jack. He used to emphasise the importance of being first to the ball on crosses and used to get me to practise it as he saw that I had a weakness in this part of my game.

'Jack used to keep a book in which he would enter all the peculiarities of the forwards he would face during a season. Whether they crossed the ball hard, floated it or cut it back, and noted from newspapers how a player had beaten a keeper from a penalty.'

United, the Cup holders, were almost knocked out right at the start of the 1951-52 campaign. They were 2-1 down to Aston Villa at St. James's in the third round with only 10 minutes to go and disillusioned fans were pouring out of the ground to wend their way home. Then Mitch took over. He struck two identical goals

Skipper Joe Harvey with the Cup is chaired by Jackie Milburn and Frank Brennan. Looking on are Bobby Corbett, Charlie Crowe, Ernie Taylor, Tommy Walker, Bobby Cowell and Bobby Mitchell.

to prick the Villa balloon and right on time George Robledo knocked in another to produce a 4-2 scoreline which had looked impossible just a few short minutes before.

Tottenham Hotspur were next at White Hart Lane. They were the League champions boasting such household names as Ted Ditchburn, Alf Ramsey, Bill Nicholson, Ron Burgess and Les Medley, but in the September United had slaughtered them 7-2 at home even without the injured Milburn. A crowd of 69,009 — many of them Geordies — packed the ground for the fourth round tie and on a mudheap of a pitch Mitchell once again proceeded to take apart the unfortunate Ramsey as United cruised home 3-0.

United beat Swansea 1-0 in Wales through a Mitchell goal to be drawn at Portsmouth in the sixth round. The stage was set for

Members of the '51 side at a reunion 30 years later. Back row: Bobby Cowell, Joe Harvey, Bobby Corbett, Charlie Crowe. Front row: Tommy Walker, Ernie Taylor, Jackie Milburn, Frank Brennan.

what will always be remembered as probably the greatest game Wor Jackie ever played for Newcastle United.

Portsmouth were a superlative side built round their international half-backs Jimmy Scoular, Jack Froggatt and Jimmy Dickinson. Before the draw United skipper Joe Harvey had said: 'We are ready for any side apart from Portsmouth at Portsmouth' and after the two were paired together Pompey boss Bob Jackson declared: 'It should be the classic of the round.' How right he was.

Pompey decided to make it their first all-ticket match at Fratton Park and the police imposed a crowd limit of 46,000. The club increased the price of terrace tickets to 2s 6d and sold them at the reserve match the previous Saturday — a wily move as it turned out, with an unbelievable crowd of 30,000 turning up to watch the stiffs bringing a windfall of £1,643 from gate receipts. The following day United put their allocation of 11,500 tickets on sale and were cleaned out in 45 minutes.

Such was the fervour on Tyneside that one fan, 56-year-old unemployed labourer Daniel Duffy from Blaydon, walked 188 of the 345 miles to Portsmouth and he didn't even have a ticket. When he arrived in the city on the Friday afternoon — his overcoat drenched and his shoes worn down — he had a halfpenny in his pocket.

'I only had cups of tea and bread and margarine in the institutes

Laura and Jackie with the Cup at the celebration dinner.

on the way down,' he declared, 'but I'll be at Fratton Park to join the Geordies in the singing of the Blaydon Races.'

The first of 10 special trains laid on for the Newcastle fans left the North East at nine o'clock on the Friday night arriving at Portsmouth and Southsea Station just after 7am on the day of the match. They were greeted by banners saying 'Welcome Newcastle' and handed leaflets on the attractions of Southsea. All the Commercial Road restaurants opened early, providing liver and

United arrive back in the Central Station in Newcastle with skipper Joe Harvey balancing the Cup on the head of little Ernie Taylor.

bacon for the Geordie hordes. About a thousand of them were allowed onto the South Parade Pier free of charge and many more rested around the Guildhall. The atmosphere was warm and friendly without a hint of malice. The exchanges between rival fans were good natured and humorous. Everyone seemed determined to enjoy the occasion, none more so than the touts. They were getting 15s for 3s 6d tickets.

By the time the gates were opened at 1pm huge queues snaked round Fratton Park. Inside the Royal Marines Band was drowned by the sound of rattles and cheers. The Geordie anthem, The Blaydon Races, thundered round the ground until the Pompey Chimes came roaring back in reply. The volume increased when little boys dressed in their teams' colours paraded round the cinder track. As the teams emerged onto the slippery pitch some supporters ran on to present players with lucky mascots.

What lay ahead was a titanic struggle between two sides both in

Wor Jackie battles with the Swansea defence in the fifth round of the Cup in 1952 at the Vetch Field.

the top five of the First Division. To recapture the epic 90 minutes let us relive the match through the eyes not of a Geordie but the local paper, the *Portsmouth Evening News:*

'Four minutes into the game Pompey went ahead. Jack Froggatt fed centre-forward Jackie Henderson, who turned it on to Peter Harris on the right wing. His instant cross split the Newcastle defence and Belgian winger Marcel Gaillard rose above Cowell to nod it in. For Froggatt, the left winger turned centre-half, that contribution was to prove a rare escape from the task of shackling the mighty Milburn. He never succeeded. For this was to be Wor Jackie's finest match.

'The game was flowing from end to end at a terrific pace with

The greatest game Wor Jackie ever played — he is seen on the ground stabbing the ball into the Portsmouth net for United's first goal at Portsmouth in the sixth round.

Milburn, arrowed, is engulfed by delirious Newcastle fans after his fabulous hat-trick against Pompey.

Milburn beats both the Blackburn Rovers right-back and goalkeeper in the semi-final.

the players making light of the treacherous surface. The first foul of any note did not arrive until the 30th minute.

'Gradually Newcastle took control. Mitchell and Tommy Walker caused havoc down both wings and shots rained in on Butler from all angles — mostly from the boot of Milburn. An earlier clash had left him holding his right hand stationary across his body but when the ball ran loose across the Pompey penalty area with five minutes of the half remaining he managed to drive home the equaliser. Before the half-time whistle blew he still had time to go off for a couple of minutes of treatment, return, and force Butler into three excellent saves.

'Within five minutes of the restart Milburn had fired in two more shots at the beleaguered Butler. Pompey battled back again but Gaillard spurned their best chance of the game when he took too much time over his shot, allowing goalkeeper Ronnie Simpson to smother the ball. Newcastle responded with venom. Robledo had a goal disallowed for offside but there was nothing wrong when Milburn netted his second in the 61st minute. Froggatt was caught in possession on his own dead ball line and Milburn was able to loop the subsequent cross over Butler.

'Again Pompey thrust forward, driven by Dickinson and Scoular. Their effort was rewarded eight minutes later when Phillips battled past a one-on-one clash with Simpson and squared it back for Reid to thump home the equaliser from close range.

'Portsmouth seemed to be gaining the upper hand when, with 10 minutes left, Milburn delivered his knock-out blow. Picking the ball up just inside his own half he burst past Froggatt and

United's Cup stars relax as Jackie plays Ronnie Simpson at table football.

veered towards the left hand corner flag. Challenged just outside the angle of the penalty area he suddenly unleashed a shot which flew across Butler and into the far corner of the net. The goal will be talked about for years. Many will wonder how Milburn managed to get the ball past Butler from such an angle and from such distance.

'The goal paralysed Pompey. They never recovered from the shock of Jackie's devastating strike and, with two minutes left, the great man laid the ball into George Robledo's path for the inside-left to fire home.'

Milburn himself looked back with affection on the 4-2 score-line and a day when he was a hero amongst heroes.

'It was the greatest match I ever played in. Every one of the 22 players gave everything they had. I was never clapped as loud as that for scoring a goal, not even when we were playing at home. It was the Pompey fans cheering as well. The match had everything: the players' attitude, the skill, the occasion, the fans. It was absolutely perfect.

'No one ever gave Jack Froggatt the runaround. He was a big pal of mine ever since we played in the England team together but it just happened to be my day that day. I was just a yard faster than him, but I had to give 100 per cent all the time. Pompey were a hell of a team and it was a hell of an achievement to go there and beat them.

'My third goal was one of my best ever. I got the ball almost on the halfway line and beat Jack Froggatt. I was on the left of the box almost 25 yards out and Jack was crafty enough to get back and narrow the angle. I knew it was going in as soon as I hit it though.

'The scenes afterwards were amazing. When we came out of the ground we could see Newcastle and Portsmouth fans, hundreds of them, linking arms and singing the Blaydon Races. It was just completely different.'

Fleet Street writers went overboard. One called Milburn 'the best centre-forward in the world' and another enthused 'I've never seen a more masterly exhibition.' Bobby Mitchell, with less masterly eloquence but a fountain of memories to call upon, merely referred to Wor Jackie's third as 'the greatest goal I have ever seen.'

United were now in the semi-finals and instead of drawing either Arsenal or Chelsea they got Second Division Blackburn Rovers but inevitably high drama still lay ahead. Rovers, with an inspirational skipper in Bill Eckersley, held Newcastle 0-0 at Sheffield before both sides moved the short distance across Yorkshire to Leeds for the replay. After 57 minutes the never ending deadlock was at last broken, Brennan feeding Milburn whose cross was headed in by Robledo. But, lo and behold, Eddie Quigley levelled things again and it was nip and tuck before, with only four minutes remaining on the clock, Robledo's header was handled on the line.

Normally there would be no problem. Milburn was United's penalty king and his would have been the honour of scoring the goal which sent the Magpies back to Wembley. But Jackie had hurt his knee earlier in the game and when skipper Harvey presented him with the ball he shied off.

'Joe told me "Come on, Jackie, do your stuff" and nearly collapsed when I replied "Not this time, Joe. My knee's playing up." For some time Joe and I argued and it must have got to

Stan Seymour and Joe Harvey lead United out against Arsenal at Wembley in 1952.

Bobby Mitchell because he picked up the ball, placed it on the spot, and looked over his shoulder at Harvey saying "I'll take it." '

The ball flew as sweet as you like past Bill Elvy and for the first time in Wembley's history the Cup holders were returning the following year to defend it.

United had only been away a year but the team changes weren't limited to Simpson for Fairbrother. Alf McMichael was in for Bobby Corbett, Ted Robledo was left-half in place of Charlie Crowe to make it two brothers in the same side, and Billy Foulkes was at inside-right for Ernie Taylor.

Playmaker Taylor had wanted to leave United after being left out of the League champions v Cup winners game and he broke a few hearts including that of Joe Harvey who loved the little fella.

'He never ran with the ball, he knocked it past people but

Jackie Milburn shakes hands with Prime Minister Winston Churchill before the game.

inevitably had it away before they could recover,' said Harvey. 'We missed his skill on the field and his clowning off it.'

Arsenal were providing the Wembley opposition this time

George Robledo, watched by No. 9 Milburn, heads the goal which beat Arsenal.

round and when the two teams were presented to Prime Minister Winston Churchill before the kick-off he smiled at Milburn and said: 'Are you going to grab the headlines again this year?'

'It really impressed me that a man like that should take notice of a pit lad,' said Milburn afterwards. King George VI, in his last Wembley final, had presented the Cup in 1951 and the Queen and Prince Philip were to do the honours in 1955. As Jackie said, not bad for a pit lad!

Early in the game the Wembley hoodoo deprived Arsenal of the services of Wally Barnes through injury but they fought a makeshift but magnificent rearguard action that kept the holders at bay until less than 10 minutes of normal time remained. Don Roper, a tearaway winger with a blistering shot, had been made into a deputy full-back in place of Barnes. Now he lay doubled in pain just outside the penalty area.

His Arsenal colleagues waved and gesticulated at referee Arthur

A proud Joe Harvey receives the trophy from Winston Churchill with Milburn in line.

Ellis but United's Bobby Mitchell was in possession, there had been no foul, and quite properly one of the outstanding officials of his time allowed play to go on. Mitchell centred into the packed goalmouth as he had done unsuccessfully so many times before on this day of agony and heroism for the Gunners.

On this occasion the unmistakable mahogany skin of George Robledo reacted with the reflexes of a cat. First a move that was an odd combination of spring and crouch, then a quick stab of the head. The ball struck the inside of the post and glanced into history.

How at that moment United must have reflected on the great piece of fortune which provided them with their goal machine.

If the nitrate workers of Iquque in Chile hadn't revolted against unemployment and misery in 1930 Mrs Robledo, a Yorkshire lass who had emigrated to Chile to be a governess and later a teacher, might never have brought her sons George, Ted and Walter to England. As the revolt spread Mrs Robledo and her children docked at Liverpool in April of 1932 and sought what she thought was temporary sanctuary in West Melton. But her husband died before a return trip could be arranged and instead two Wembley footballers were to emerge.

Packed streets in Newcastle welcome back the Cup heroes.

Milburn, who always hated playing against 10 men, was far-seeing enough to call for substitutes after United's victory — something which is commonplace now, of course.

After the final, United went on tour to South Africa and received permission from the F.A. to take the Cup out of Britain for the first time.

'The tour lasted 10 weeks and for the first five I couldn't play,' said Jackie. 'I was left at base with director Wally Hurford while the lads gallivanted all over the veldt. I had taken a kick from Don Roper in the final and needed constant attention from specialists. The following season, as it happened, I suffered the only really serious injury of my career which resulted in a cartilage operation. But I was back playing again in less than six weeks. I wouldn't have done so, only director William McKeag, a man I respected, asked me to have a run-out in the third team at Wallsend and promised me 'a little something' for supposedly adding a bit of glamour to the match. As it happened I got nothing — not that I wanted anything in the first place — but my appearance caused more than a spot of bother. Twelve thousand folk turned up to watch us on a tiny ground designed to hold about twelve hundred. We won 2-1, with me scoring one of the goals, but this sparked off violent protests from the opposition who would have won the league title but for that defeat.'

Looking back on the tour Jackie recalled: 'Frank Brennan was never bothered much about appearances and he turned up for the trip to South Africa with a toothbrush in his top pocket and nowt else. He was presented with a Zulu spear the moment he arrived and spent the entire 10 weeks travelling around the country with a toothbrush in one hand and his spear in the other. He borrowed shaving gear from me, vests from George Robledo and socks from Mitch.'

Brennan was capable of picking up an opponent by the scruff of the neck with one huge hand and shaking him as a terrier shakes a rat. His fellow Scot Ronnie Simpson says of his old room-mate: 'There were times when he virtually carried us on his huge shoulders. I never played against or with a better centre-half. He had absolutely no nerves whatsoever on the field. He never flustered, never panicked. He slept like a baby, without a care in the world and then would go out and play to the crowd. He loved their hero worship.'

Brennan had a host of nicknames . . . the Rock of Gibraltar, the Ambling Alp, Bren Gun. In short he was a character but sadly he left United before their next Cup-winning feat, banished into non-league soccer over a row about him opening a sports shop. There were protest meetings and letters flooded into the *Evening Chronicle* but it was the end of a remarkable career.

CHAPTER NINE

Wembley Revisited

Two years passed before United again turned their sights on Wembley Way; two years in which things changed dramatically. Gone were Joe Harvey into retirement, the Robledos back to Chile, Brennan into obscurity and Walker to Oldham. A new controversial manager, Duggie Livingstone, was in charge and players like old Portsmouth foe Jimmy Scoular, Ron Batty, Bob Stokoe, Len White, Vic Keeble and George Hannah had emerged into the side.

Only three players — Wor Jackie, Mitch and Bobby Cowell — were to play in all three finals. And even then Milburn almost didn't make it though we mustn't get ahead of ourselves.

The early steps were tentative . . . a third round win at Plymouth Argyle by 1-0 due in no small measure to Simpson's sharp reflexes on an icy pitch and a good goal from Keeble, and victory over Brentford 3-2 at St. James's in another close encounter. Then came a marathon against Nottingham Forest. It took United five hours and thirty minutes to dispose of them over three games.

With first White and then Keeble wearing the famed No. 9 shirt throughout the season Milburn was confined to either outside-right or inside-left as he battled throughout to overcome a pulled stomach muscle, a bad injury for a footballer. But at Forest in the first match Jackie once again proved, if it were necessary, that he was still a match winner of the highest quality. Or, in this case, a match saver.

United's three Wembley programmes of the fifties.

'Jackie scored a pile of goals in his career, many of them spectacular, but he told me the most satisfying one ever was at the City Ground,' said brother-in-law Les Common. 'United were losing 1-0 with only 90 seconds to go when the ball was knocked to Jack inside his own half. His first inclination was to turn it to Mitch but instead he set off on his own. He got past one of the wing-halves and out of the corner of his eye could see the two full-backs converging on him. He knew that time wasn't on his side, that if he shot over the bar and a goal kick was taken it would be the end of the match.

'Jackie waited and waited and then, just as he slid the ball home, both full-backs hit him simultaneously. His thigh was red raw — but Newcastle were still in the Cup.'

In the replay at St. James's United thought they themselves had the match won, leading as they were 2-0 at half-time with Mitchell and Keeble the marksmen. But plucky Forest fought back to score twice before the 90 minutes were up and extra time couldn't part the two of them. The first attempt to play the game had fallen foul of the diabolical winter's weather and labourers had been forced to clear fifteen inches of snow from the pitch to eventually get the replay under way.

A flip of a coin to decide the venue took the second replay back to St. James's and, believe it or not, extra time was needed once again before United inched through 2-1. Alan Monkhouse, a reserve centre-forward in for the injured Keeble, had the glory of scoring both goals but they were each made by Milburn, who had a fine match.

If United were getting Cup weary as game upon game piled up, then it didn't show. Round six brought a 1-1 draw at First Division Huddersfield Town with a late close-in equaliser by Len White, and the St. James's replay was 104 minutes old before Mitchell broke the stranglehold for Keeble to add No. 2 six minutes later.

Mitch, master of the dribble with a left foot as precious as gold, had paralysed Huddersfield's right-back Ron Staniforth who had been a member of England's World Cup squad only the year before.

If United met Third Division opposition in the semi-final then, true to pattern, it still took them an extra game to get through to Wembley. York City had beaten the might of Spurs and Blackpool to go so close and they almost added the name of United to their giant-killing in the first tie at Hillsborough. It ended 1-1 with Keeble, by now into his goalscoring stride, hitting the net again. But a replay at Roker Park, Sunderland was almost like a home tie for the Magpies who clinched it 2-0 — an early White picture goal and a typical Keeble header in the dying minutes.

Wembley for the third time in five years lay but weeks ahead. Yet United, their supporters, and the whole country were to be rocked by one of the biggest sensations of any Cup final week. Duggie Livingstone, a manager who courted controversy and new fangled ideas, actually dropped Milburn from his Wembley team. The same Milburn who had scored two stunning goals in the 1951 final, the same Milburn who was back a year later, and the same Milburn who had first saved United against Nottingham Forest and then provided the ammunition to destroy them. Wor Jackie, already a Cup legend whose very presence could strike fear into the most staunch of hearts.

Parting Milburn from Wembley in the early 50s was like thinking of The Derby without Lester Piggott, England's Test side without Len Hutton or Wimbledon without Lew Hoad. The directors, and Stan Seymour in particular, were horrified.

On the Monday before United's party departed for traditional

A ticket for the 1955 final priced 3s 6d.

Cup training at Brighton the drama unfolded when Livingstone told Len White he would be playing at Wembley. It meant Milburn was out but two days later, after the board had been informed, Seymour tore up Livingstone's team sheet and chucked it in the nearest wastepaper bin. Milburn was back in and White was 12th man. But there was still to be an ironic twist — on the eve of the big game inside-forward Reg Davies went down with tonsillitis so White the yo-yo man was called up on the right wing with Jackie inside him.

It had all been tacky and disruptive and was to spell the end for Livingstone who left a few months later.

'Frankly, I had little respect for Livingstone,' admitted Milburn. 'I remember him once in training putting a chalk mark on Bobby Mitchell's boot showing him how to sidefoot a ball properly. Magical Mitch, of all people, probably the best placer of a ball we had. And he told me I didn't strike the ball properly when shooting.

'He'd worked in Sweden and came in bristling with new coaching techniques. He had us jumping over high hurdles then ducking under them and leaping into the air to head the ball. After the first week there were no fewer than 10 players on the treatment table with groin strains. We needed new training like a hole in the head — we were naturals and all the new techniques simply upset the balance. That at least was the view of the older players although some of the younger ones went along with the revolution and for the first time there was a rift in the club. Cliques began to appear.

'Fortunately he had made Joe Harvey coach for the 1955 Cup run and that saved us because he was able to bridge the gap between the senior players and the manager. We all thought the world of Joe and he used to say "Forget everything else, it's up to you lot on the field. You decide what really happens." '

Just before the Cup final Seymour whispered to Milburn: 'Go out and show them, Jackie' and within 45 seconds — yes, seconds — he had done just that. Newcastle won a corner on the right and when White arrowed it towards the near post, Milburn, left unmarked by Manchester City captain Roy Paul, rose like a salmon to head the ball unerringly past Bert Trautmann. As the ball fizzed against the back of the rigging Livingstone must have been squirming in his seat. It was the fastest goal in Wembley's history.

Actually there was no animosity between Milburn and White over the Wembley team selection. They both respected each other's ability. Jackie was to call White 'the best uncapped centre-forward United ever had' and Len told me: 'Jackie was a gentleman and an outstanding player. We had a lot of fun together — I remember once in the Great Northern Hotel at King's Cross we were larking about and Jack bet me I couldn't walk on my hands over the tables for a second time. I did it but right at the end I slipped, somersaulted, and the shade off a nearby lampstand fell perfectly over my head. On the train journey home the club tried to find out for hours who did the damage but I never owned up and they paid. I didn't want the kids to live on grass sandwiches for the rest of the week.'

White insisted that his early corner was actually a bad kick turned into a good one by Milburn. He admitted he intended to play it to the back post for the head of the lethal Keeble but understruck it for Jackie to head home brilliantly.

Bert Trautmann, Manchester City's keeper, collects a high ball challenged by Jackie Milburn.

From then on the Wembley show was run by right-half Scoular and left winger Mitchell. Long sweeping passes from Scoular to Mitch ripped the heart out of City who, like Arsenal in 1952, lost a full-back Jimmy Meadows through injury. But this time, even though City fleetingly levelled things, further Newcastle goals from Mitchell and George Hannah brought a thoroughly deserved 3-1 victory.

Seymour, totally vindicated, proudly watched the match from the Royal Box, sitting between the Queen and Princess Margaret.

When Bobby Cowell made an uncharacteristic blunder Seymour moaned: 'Oh Bobby, use yer nut, man.'

Princess Margaret, turning to Stan, inquired: 'Excuse me, Mr Seymour, but what is your nut?' A rather flustered Newcastle director explained that nut was a Geordie term for brains.

At the end, with the Geordies merrily singing the Blaydon Races, Princess Margaret turned again to Stan.

'Congratulations, Mr Seymour,' she said, 'and I'll remember to use my nut in the future!'

Jackie and Laura proudly look at a picture of Milburn's fastest-ever goal, scored after just 45 seconds of the 1955 final against Manchester City.

Milburn's greatest moments were now complete and he viewed them with the passing of time this way: 'In my day you played football out of a mixture of pride and love. Superstar salaries hadn't been invented and, looking back, I suppose our wages were on the low side, especially considering all the folk we entertained and the huge, huge crowds. Len Shackleton always thought so, anyway, but he was ahead of his time.

'The cash honestly didn't matter that much to me. I wouldn't have swapped my experiences for all the gold in Fort Knox. For winning three Cup finals I received less than £80 including bonuses. My weekly wage was £12 in the winter and £8 in the summer and whenever we won a match there was a £2 bonus all round. "Come on, lads", Joe Harvey used to say, "it's time to get the groceries" and he was right. Most of the bonus did get spent on little extras for the wife and the kids.'

The worth of Wor Jackie to Newcastle United in the early '50s

George Hannah scores United's third to clinch the Cup.

was underlined by Ronnie Simpson, who watched the '51 triumph from the stands and played in '52 and '55.

'He belonged to Newcastle as Newcastle belonged to him. He was a real broad Geordie who understood the fans and he was their idol. United didn't look the same when Jackie wasn't in the side and I think the crowd at St. James's Park felt the same. He was such a wonderful personality and such a match winner. He was also unorthodox as most great players are. He used to lean back and crack 'em low into the corner of the net. It fooled most goalkeepers as you always expect the ball to rise when you see a forward leaning backwards.'

Vic Keeble, his final Wembley partner, never possessed the all-round ability of Milburn, being strictly limited on the ground, but he recognised the worth of the man at his shoulder.

'No one needs telling what a tremendous player he was, the power he possessed in either foot, the fantastic pace he had. Honestly, there wouldn't be the money to buy him today. Jack was a great player but an even better person. Unfortunately the likes of him only pass this way once and we are unlikely to see the sort of talent that he had again in our lifetime.'

The Cup exploits over, there was one ironic, yet faintly amusing, tailpiece.

'There was to be a celebration dance at the Oxford Galleries in the centre of town and our wives were to be presented with handbags which, it was rumoured, would be stuffed full of cash,' Milburn told me. 'Fair dues, you might think, considering that we had made the club rich through our endeavours and players' wages were peanuts. Boy, did we look forward to the quickstep — we hadn't looked for the cash but we'd gratefully accept it. Come the big night we all sat there trying to conceal our delight as one by one by one our wives trooped up to the bandstand. The handbags they were given were bulging to almost obscene proportions and, in fact, the strap of Mrs George Hannah's bag snapped as she was carrying it back to her table. A dozen pair of eyes registered the same thought: "It's the weight. Whoopee!"

'With a nonchalant air the lads remarked how beautiful the bags were, then, hardly able to contain themselves, grabbed them and ripped them open. Each one was stuffed with newspaper. Not a sign of the green crinkly stuff anywhere.

'Looking back, we must have been quite a sight sitting up to our knees in crumpled newspaper, but I don't remember being particularly amused at the time. To make matters worse we later learned that the club had bought a job lot of about 30 bags for seventeen quid!'

No one would doubt Milburn's place in Cup history. How could they? Three winner's medals and three superb goals tell their own tale of romance and achievement. But what may not be fully realised is that Wor Jackie is officially the greatest ever centre-forward to play in the biggest domestic competition of the lot.

Back in 1981 the Football Association immortalised the all-time greats of 100 Cup finals to mark the centenary of their prestige event. Twelve solid silver cigarette cards depicting the best players in each position — plus a sub — were struck. And Wor Jackie was named in the most romantic of all positions, centre-forward.

A limited edition of 2,000 were produced selling at £260 a set and have become collectors' items. Ironically, two of the players who tasted execution by the flashing blade of Milburn — Blackpool winger Stanley Matthews and Manchester City goalkeeper Bert Trautmann — still became silver heroes. Matthews, of course, for the 1953 Cup final when he at last gained a winner's medal and the former German prisoner of war for defying a

Captain Jimmy Scoular comes down the steps from the Royal Box with the trophy.

broken neck in his successful glory bid in 1956, the year after Wor Jackie decimated him with his goal after only 45 seconds. Milburn fictionally lined up with Raich Carter, Sunderland's 1937 winning captain who had such an impact on him when he attended his first ever soccer match at the impressionable age of 13, and Bobby Charlton, a fully paid up member of the Milburn clan.

The 11 Cup superstars were Trautmann (Manchester City); Spencer (Aston Villa), Hapgood (Arsenal); D. Blanchflower (Spurs), Wright (Wolves), Moore (West Ham); Matthews (Blackpool), Carter (Sunderland), Milburn (Newcastle United), B. Charlton (Manchester United), Finney (Preston). Duncan Edwards, that giant of a boy who would have won so much with

Manchester United but for the horrific Munich Air Disaster, was named as sub.

What a team. What a forward line. And what a centre-forward.

CHAPTER TEN

The Man Behind A Legend

There are two ways of accepting stardom. Malcolm Macdonald, who followed Wor Jackie into both the Newcastle and England sides, revelled in it. He smoked cigars, drank champagne and loved nightclubs. The trappings of fame rested easily on his broad shoulders. His was one way of coping with the pressures of being constantly in the public eye. But Milburn was no extrovert. Basically a shy man who got embarrassed by fan worship (while still being flattered), he opted for a second way of contending with a tricky problem.

Simply his shyness took him into a shell. While polite and courteous, he hid away whenever possible. It was that much easier than going red and mumbling through your embarrassment.

'Honest, I was scared to death to play football on the beach with the kids like other dads did. I was embarrassed. I felt people would be watching. I'd prefer to hide away behind a rock. Perhaps it was silly but it was a real problem nonetheless. I knew I was public property and I never resented that. After all, ordinary folk paid my wages. But I still found it hard to be a showman off the park. It didn't come naturally.'

Even in Ashington amongst his mates it was tricky. Simple things we all enjoy like going to the beach or the cinema became a problem.

Jackie's answer was to book a couple of aisle seats at the pictures — you could in those days — and slip in under the cover of darkness. His brother-in-law Les Common would go in normally while Milburn was parking the car, then he'd nip in five minutes after the main film was showing.

'We used to go to the Buffalo in Ashington and the manager always gave Jackie the same two seats by the aisle so it was easy for him to find them in the dark,' said Les. 'Then, with five minutes of the film left, Jackie would be off again to bring the car round. He never saw the beginning or end of a picture and I had to fill him in on the way home as to what had happened. It was pure shyness. He knew if he'd have walked in with everyone else they wouldn't even have started the film until all the clamour was over.'

When Jack first hit the big time sweets were still rationed. You could only get them with coupons — but the local Italian ice cream parlour used to look after their most famous customer.

'Jack would come back armed with Mars bars, toffees, chocolate, the lot for me to guzzle during the show. It was champion. I could have put on a stone in weight!'

Milburn was never a nightclubber or even a regular visitor to his local social club like so many of his mates in the mines. His was the quiet life at home listening to the crooners who were the singing stars of his time. His favourite record in later life was Bing Crosby's 'That Sly Old Gentleman,' a song he'd sung in one of his films to a child sitting in the back of a car. From the age of two his grand-daughter Laura knew every word.

A get together at his mother's house in Ashington on a Saturday night was a regular occurrence just after Jackie joined United.

'I remember Colin Gibson, who went on to be a star at Aston Villa, sitting at the piano and we were in full voice,' said Common. 'They were nights full of fun and good nature. You made your own entertainment in those days and Jack used to bring a lot of the lads through.'

Jackie's sister Jean recalls those times vividly. 'When he came home from the match there was always a post mortem on the game every Saturday night. I don't think our Jack liked it very much but his dad used to go through every move and we had a houseful of his friends until two and three o'clock in the morning. Sometimes it was a sing song or perhaps a game of darts.'

Jackie and Laura with Linda, Jackie junior and Betty pictured at home in 1956.

The family were stunned when Jack announced he was to marry a girl he had met on an away trip with Newcastle.

'It must have been love at first sight,' says Jean. 'When he came back and told us we couldn't believe it. Jack wasn't the impulsive type and it seemed out of character. But as soon as we met her everybody liked her. I shall always be thankful to Laura for looking after our Jack the way she did. She was always behind him, she was there all the time.'

The one thing Milburn did inherit from his Ashington background was his love of dog racing. He'd attend greyhound meetings at Portland Park or in the Newcastle city centre at Brough Park. He even had a greyhound named after him.

'Jackie wasn't a big betting man but he loved the excitement and the atmosphere of a dog track,' remembers Common. 'He'd only have a small flutter but the characters fascinated him.'

Raymond Poxton, the lad who went for a trial with Wor Jackie to St. James's Park, saw at first hand how the love of the chase gripped a young Milburn.

'For a while football took second place to greyhounds. I helped to persuade him that soccer should come first but Jack always maintained his interest in the dogs. It was the excitement of it all. It was funny the fascination that he had because as a footballer he was often likened to a greyhound, such was his speed.'

Old mates recall Jackie as a quiet lad with no airs and graces.

'He wasn't a snob,' maintained Ronnie Coulson. 'He always remembered his own folk. He was just an ordinary lad.'

Another pal Joe Smith, who knew him intimately from the age of 12 until 21, told me: 'Jack wasn't a boozer or a great socialiser though he liked his fags. We went to school together and were apprentices together at the local pit. Jack was just one of the boys.

'In those days with the war biting it was difficult to get hold of things and one day when I was in the Co-op one of the assistants told me they had a pair of brand-new football boots so naturally I took them. They were half a size too big for me but they fitted Jackie like a glove.

'When the advert appeared in the *North Mail* asking for trialists to go through to Newcastle United, Raymond Poxton and Jackie replied and Jack asked at work the following morning if he could borrow my boots. He said he'd break them in for me. They were never off his feet after that — he would dubbin them and belt balls all over the place to get the right feel. Eventually he played his trial in them and we all know what happened after that. I was proud later to think that Jackie had made it in a pair of boots borrowed from me.'

Joe stayed close to Jackie during those early days when he tentatively tried to climb the ladder of success and once when he was injured and unable to get through to St. James's for treatment he actually helped him get fit back home in Ashington.

'His dad, Alec, used to call me Jackie's trainer.'

Milburn, highly successful as a footballer, didn't quite take the same expertise with him into the business world. He tried many things as a player — manager of a fireplace shop, proprietor of a coach firm and a showbiz agency booking acts into local clubs — all without huge success. His genius lay in his boots.

Les Common summed it up this way: 'He wasn't that sort of fella. His biggest fault was his generosity. He loved to give people things and that's not a good criterion to take into the business world.'

Jack and Laura had three children . . . first came Linda, then a year later Betty and finally, two years further on, Jackie Junior. Life can be hard growing up in the shadow of a famous father but when the door was closed in the Milburn household Jackie was merely dad. And there were moments of fun in the fame. Take the day Wor Jackie took the F.A. Cup back to Ellington Terrace in Ashington following the 1955 triumph over Manchester City.

'We stood it in the corner of the room while everyone rabbited on about the victory,' Milburn told me. 'We were much too excited to notice Betty, a toddler at the time, drag the Cup outside. The first we knew was when we heard shouts from the backlane. "Daddy, daddy," she was calling. "Look what I'm doing." When I got out there I couldn't believe my eyes. That lovely silver pot, everyone's pride and joy, was caked in dirt and full to the brim of the most disgusting mixture you've ever seen.

' "I'm making mud pies," explained Betty triumphantly, arms up to the elbows in liquid mud and squelching the stuff through her fingers. We all stood horrified with thoughts of the Cup being defaced for life but it's amazing what a bit of elbow grease can do. Every time I saw a skipper at Wembley raise the Cup aloft after that I thought about Betty and the mudpies!'

Laura recalls Jackie both as a famous footballer and in retirement as 'never changing. He was the same man from the very first day I met him. Jack was a home bird who hated anyone making a fuss of him. Yet little things pleased him and I remember how thrilled he was with his last two presentations just before he died — a gift from his fellow journalists in the Football Writers Association and the Wilkinson Sword of Honour presented by the Duke of Edinburgh at the Newcastle Civic Centre for his services to football. They still have pride of place in our living-room.'

Jack ended up a grandad six times over — Betty had four kids and Linda two. And he was in his element.

'Jack took Betty's youngest Laura all over with him and she misses him terribly, Laura told me. A year after he died she suddenly said "I wish I was still six." When I asked why she replied "because grandpa would still be here." '

He would also take another of Betty's kids, John, to the football matches at St. James's when he was working for a national newspaper. They would both write their reports of the game and compare them on a Saturday night.

Perhaps it was his sister Jean who summed up Jackie Milburn succinctly. 'I was very proud of my brother. He was a lovely man. I couldn't have asked for more.'

CHAPTER ELEVEN

Off to Ireland

Perhaps it was appropriate that Jackie Milburn never played for any other Football League club than Newcastle United. It would have seemed wrong somehow if he had shed his black and white plumage to return to St. James's Park in the finery of another club. It would probably have been difficult for him to take and certainly difficult for the fans to accept that Milburn was no longer 'Wor Jackie.'

There had been a couple of transfer requests of course — through a long career at a single club there had to be. But Jackie's heart was never really in leaving for other parts of the country. They were merely storms in a tea cup. However, all good things must come to an end and Jackie remembered the old stage adage: always leave 'em wanting more. His father, Alec, had urged him before he died: 'Don't outstay your welcome, son.'

So in June of 1957 with his greatest days at Newcastle now behind him Milburn decided to cut his ties and go off to Belfast and the gentler demands of the Irish League as Linfield's player-coach.

The burden of a three-times Cup winning and goalscoring centre-foward is heavy and needs young legs. Jackie didn't want to tarnish that image, to have doting fathers take along their young sons to see 'the great Milburn' and merely witness a pale shadow of his former self.

Jackie was now 33 years of age and knew he could play on at a certain level. In fact a glittering short career lay ahead of him in the Emerald Isle which would, eventually, only add to his charisma and standing. A whole new band of fans were to revere him as 'Our Jackie.'

Milburn had completed two more seasons with United after his third Cup victory — 1955-56 and 1956-57 — and actually won a belated 13th England cap against Denmark four years after his last before his days in stripes were officially over.

No one scored more goals for United than Jackie, whose record still stands proudly in the annals of the club. But Les Common insisted: 'Jack was as much a maker of goals as a taker. When I stood on the terraces we used to have bets with the rival fans around us on the first goalscorer. I well remember Jackie giving Burnley centre-half Tommy Cummings a right runaround. On the first goal Milburn did everything including beating the keeper and then rolled the ball for George Robledo to tap it into the net.

'The fan who had Robledo's name said: "I can't claim the goal. It really was Milburn's". And so it went on. United won by six goals and Jackie didn't score one of them but he was always involved.'

When Jackie signed for Linfield in June of 1957 what lay ahead perhaps even he could never have imagined. League titles, cups, player of the year awards and a first ever appearance in the newly formed European Cup were all to be his. It was as though nature had opened up a second career for a player who had already scaled Everest.

Malcolm Brodie, the distinguished sports editor of the *Belfast Evening Telegraph*, charted Milburn's short but spectacular career across the Irish Sea and has no doubt about his place in Irish soccer history despite the passing of the years.

'Without any doubt Jackie Milburn was the greatest crowd pulling player in the history of Irish football either in the north or the south,' he told me. 'An appearance by Jackie immediately put 5,000 on the gate. He was idolised not only by Linfield fans but everyone throughout Northern Ireland.

'He was the greatest goalscorer I've ever seen in Irish soccer and I haven't missed a Northern Ireland international match home or away anywhere in the world since 1944. Not only was he an outstanding player but he showed his sporting qualities here as well.

Signing on — Jackie puts pen to paper to join Linfield in 1957.

Ireland have a number of sporting heroes and I rank Jackie at the very top along with that legendary rugby star Jackie Kyle.

'He was the sort of man any mother or father would put forward as an example for their son to follow. It was with deep sadness that we finally saw him leave for England again but right up to his death he remained an idol in this country.'

Brodie recalls the birth of the idea to try and sign Wor Jackie, an improbable pipedream which became a glorious reality.

'It all began when Newcastle United played at Linfield to open the Windsor Park floodlights. Jackie was in the directors' box with Dick Keith who joined United from Linfield in September of 1956. Dick said to him "How would you like to play here, Jackie?"

'Milburn replied: "I wouldn't mind at all." That conversation was overheard and the seed was sown. Then some months later Jackie and his wife Laura came to Belfast for a short period and he agreed to play in two benefit games. He trained at Windsor Park along with Dick Keith and as he lapped the track Linfield secretary Joe Mackey declared: "He's the man for us." An approach was made to Stan Seymour and the outcome was Jackie's signing.'

The game to mark the opening of Linfield's lights took place on October 10, 1956 with United winning 4-1 in front of a big crowd of 35,000. Milburn scored a peach of a goal reviving memories in the Belfast faithful of his four goals back in 1948 when Linfield were beaten 6-0 at the start of an unbeaten tour of Ireland.

If there was a twinge of sadness at leaving United it was mainly because of the method of his departure.

'United asked for £20,000 plus an inside-forward called Jimmy Hill in part exchange which I thought was pretty thick after my years of loyal service. They were skinning the club I was joining and consequently leaving no money in the Linfield coffers for me to buy new players.

'Despite being only a part-time club Linfield offered me a club house, £25 a week and a £1,000 signing-on fee which had considerable attraction. My top whack with United as their England centre-forward was £17 a week so I decided, with something of a heavy heart, to cut the ties and cross the Irish sea.

'It's funny how Ireland had kept figuring in my career. My first representative honour was against the Irish League and my first England cap against Ireland, both scoring debuts.'

Milburn and Seymour spent 15 hours getting to Belfast by land and sea — now it would take one hour 45 minutes to fly door to door — and when they arrived Jackie duly signed a five-year contract as player-coach in the private room of an hotel where the Press had been invited to an informal cocktail party. Then it was off to a civic reception in the beautiful Belfast City Hall. Linfield were already beating the gong.

A month later when he arrived permanently in Ireland 'I found bands were playing, the flags were flutterng in the warm summer breeze, and thousands of people were thronging the streets around Lisburn Road. I couldn't believe they were doing all this for me — then someone told me it was the Twelfth of July! As an uninformed Englishman I hadn't a clue about the significance of the date.'

Over the next three and a half years, however, Milburn was to receive incredible welcomes like that everywhere he went with

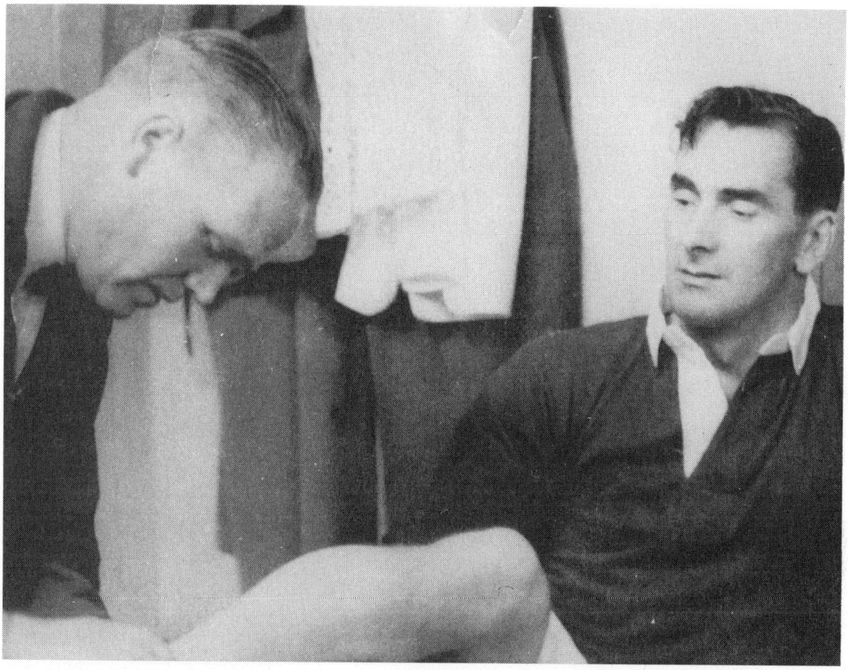

Jackie receives treatment from Linfield trainer Jimmy McCune.

Linfield. He was feted as a true star. Jackie had a magnetic effect on Irish League football with his penchant for scoring spectacular goals. He got six in a 9-0 win over Crusaders, two in the Irish Cup final win over Ards and he piloted Linfield, known locally as the Blues, to nine trophies — the City Cup, Gold Cup and Co. Antrim Shield in 1957-58; Irish League, City Cup and Co. Antrim Shield in 1958-59; Irish Cup, Gold Cup and Ulster Cup in 1959-60 and he was in the Linfield team beaten 2-0 by Ballymena in the 1957-58 Irish Cup final. He scored on every ground except Mourneview Park.

Jackie was Ulster Footballer of the Year in 1957-58 and twice the League's leading scorer with 55 goals in 1957-58 and 56 in 1958-59. Add to that a historic goalscoring appearance in the European Cup and selection for the Irish League against the Football League and the mind goes blurred at the welter of honours.

Yet Milburn maintained: 'I had to play deeper than I did at Newcastle and my initial reaction was that the game was slower than in England with players wanting to dribble with the ball

Wor Jackie receives his Irish Footballer of the Year trophy in 1958 from Jim Morgan (left).

before parting. But there were good players in the Irish League. Wilbur Cush was outstanding before he went over to Leeds and on my debut at Distillery I was fascinated by a kid playing at inside-forward who waltzed through the game. His name was Derek Dougan.'

Jackie's love affair with United continued during his exile.

'I regularly flew from Belfast to either Newcastle or London to watch United play and always paid the air fare out of my own pocket. They still meant that much to me. Once I agreed to join the lads in Manchester before a game against City. The only plane available at short notice was one travelling to Australia with a load of pigs but the pilot agreed to take me to Liverpool from where I could easily drop down the road into Manchester. So there was Jackie Milburn, sitting in the back surrounded by pigs as the pilot sang "Three little girls sitting in the back seat" at the top of his voice.

Jackie Milburn in the strip of the Irish League.

'When I arrived in Manchester manager Charlie Mitten was delighted to see me. Perhaps just a little bit too delighted. He greeted me like a long lost brother and told the directors: "Get the lads in the coach and off you go. We'll get a taxi to the ground later — I want to talk to Jackie." In fact it turned out he had a bet on the two o'clock race and wanted to watch it on telly. He'd just been wondering what excuse to give when I turned up and provided one for him.'

Mitten actually wrote to Milburn suggesting he should re-sign for Newcastle, a staggering switch had it come off. The idea was sparked off by Jackie's performance for the Irish League against the Football League at Blackpool.

'The opposition included foreigners such as John White, Danny Blanchflower and Denis Law and though they beat us right enough I had a blinder and suddenly, at the age of almost 36, I found myself in demand again. I received a host of offers to return to the big time but, having drawn my £600 provident money, I was barred.'

Milburn also played other games for the Irish League, drawing a crowd of 25,000 in Dublin against the League of Ireland — a match which ended in a 2-2 draw — and then the following month at Cliftonville in the return he injured his right leg during the first-half and limped for the rest of the game. But seven minutes from the end, taking a clearance by his own keeper Russell on the halfway line, he shrugged off the injury to go on one of his blazing runs which ended with a scorching shot to clinch a 3-1 victory.

It was in the same year — 1958 — that Wor Jackie participated in his second World Cup. A player with England in 1950, this time Linfield paid for him to join the Northern Ireland party for the finals in Sweden. The idea was for their player-coach to study the techniques, tactics and training but he did much more than that.

'Peter Doherty and Danny Blanchflower knew the value of Jackie and they used him as a spy,' Malcolm Brodie told me. 'He looked at Northern Ireland's future opposition — Czechoslovakia, Argentina and West Germany — and on the basis of his reports the Irish stall was set out.'

Little Ireland, backed by the Milburn plan, created the pattern for future World Cup exploits, beating the Czechs in Halmstad through Wilbur Cush's solitary goal, drawing 2-2 with West Germany and losing to Argentina to qualify for the play-offs.

Milburn at his desk at Windsor Park, Belfast.

Their team included Jackie's former Newcastle team-mates Dick Keith, Alf McMichael and Tommy Casey, the magnificent Harry Gregg in goal, Danny Blanchflower's creativity, winger Peter McParland, Billy Bingham, Jimmy McIlroy and young Derek Dougan.

While Scotland had been eliminated three British sides — England, Wales and Northern Ireland — took part in the play-off games to try and get through to the quarter-finals. England were surprisingly beaten by Russia in Gothenburg but Northern Ireland and Wales gained dramatic extra time victories. The Welsh eliminated Hungary in Stockholm while the plucky Irish overcame a Czech side which was fresh from swamping Argentina. Both Gregg and Casey were missing, with Jackie Scott gaining his first cap. Deputy keeper Norman Uprichard was injured and so was Bertie Peacock. Czechoslovakia took the lead, the game went into extra time and still Ireland won.

McParland had equalised and nine minutes into extra time he volleyed home Danny Blanchflower's free-kick.

Ireland, wearied by a 210-mile coach journey to Norrkoping

plus the absence of Peacock with torn ligaments and the need to play the damaged Casey, blew up against France while Wales, without John Charles, went down to Brazil, the eventual winners. But the Irish had died magnificently and Milburn had played a full part in their achievements.

The wider stage was the sort on which Wor Jackie loved to perform and there was one more dramatic appearance still to be made. European cup football was a door never open to him during his barnstorming days with United. The winning of the F.A. Cup would have meant automatic entry to the European Cupwinners' Cup in later years but that vision had yet to become a reality. At Linfield, however, Jackie made a belated but inevitably effective entrance to the European scene.

By the summer of 1959 Milburn was already looking towards England. He had loved his years in the Emerald Isle but new pastures, new mountains to be climbed, tempted him. He asked Linfield to release him from his five-year contract to return home.

It was a crippling blow to the little part-time club. The thought of losing not only their player-coach but the greatest crowd puller in the land, not to mention the greatest goalscorer, was like someone suddenly pulling down the blinds. The sunlight had vanished forever.

But they realised Milburn was serious and, because of the dignity he had shown throughout his stay, they decided to reluctantly play ball. But a compromise was reached — Jackie would hang on for three months to play in Linfield's European Cup two-legged tie with Swedish champions Gothenburg.

'The match captured the imagination of Belfast and 41,000 turned up at Windsor Park to see us pull off a magnificent 2-1 win,' said Jack. 'I scored both our goals, which was nice considering age meant I wouldn't play in Europe's No. 1 competition again, but in the return the Swedes decided I was the danger man and kicked me up in the air. We lost 6-1 but no one could take away the joy of the Belfast result.'

Behind him lay forever this magnificent record as a Magpie:

	LEAGUE		*F.A. CUP*		*WARTIME*		*TOTAL*	
	App.	*Gls.*	*App.*	*Gls.*	*App.*	*Gls.*	*App.*	*Gls*
1943-44					24	12	24	12
1944-45					32	12	32	12
1945-46			2	2	39	14	41	16
1946-47	24	7	3	1			27	8
1947-48	39	20	1				40	20
1948-49	34	19	1				35	19
1949-50	30	18	2	3			32	21
1950-51	31	17	8	8			39	25
1951-52	32	25	7	3			39	28
1952-53	16	5					16	5
1953-54	39	16	5	2			44	18
1954-55	38	19	10	2			48	21
1955-56	38	19	4	2			42	21
1956-57	32	12	1				33	12
	353	177	44	23	95	38	492	238

CHAPTER TWELVE

Football League Manager

News that Milburn was heading back across the sea alerted Ashington, then still a strong non-league club playing in the Midland League. Wouldn't it be nice to have their home town boy as player-manager? What a triumphant return for the former ball boy to Portland Park!

The Sunday Pictorial, now defunct, carried a story forecasting: 'Everything's ready for him to sign on the dotted line for £25-£30 a week. He would put £70-£80 on the gate of his home town club.

'Ashington chairman Bill Nunn says: "I'm confident we'll get him." '

Confident, maybe, but they didn't really know Jackie Milburn. Sure, he had talks. He listened courteously. He was tempted. But he said no.

Later he explained: 'I never used to watch United when I wasn't playing. Instead I went down to Portland Park to watch the locals. One day I saw Len Duns, who had won the First Division championship and the F.A. Cup with Sunderland, getting the bird from the crowd. He was over the hill a little and consequently not as sharp as he used to be. But it seemed sacrilege to me that a player of his calibre should be subjected to such abuse. So when the chance came for me to join Ashington I politely refused. The fans remembered me as Wor Jackie, the speed merchant with bombs in his boots. I didn't want to tarnish that image. I was afraid.'

Other local sides nibbled, of course. There were North Shields and South Shields, both members of the Northern Counties League, and Berwick Rangers, playing over the border in Scotland. But Milburn wasn't to come back to the North East.

'I felt my apprenticeship was over at Linfield. So the best move was to get as near to London as possible and get in on the action. That's why I became player-manager of Yiewsley Town and it worked because I eventually landed the manager's job at First Division Ipswich Town.'

Jackie spent two years with the prosperous Southern League club which included London Airport in its town boundaries, had a 40,000 capacity ground, floodlights and a concert hall 100 feet long. With a North Easterner as chairman, Alf Whittit from Sunderland, and a sprinkling of Geordies on the books, Milburn settled in quickly to lift a club which had only been professional for two years up the league, hitting the back of the net just as he had done so regularly in the big time.

He also capitalised on his short stay by working fleetingly at Third Division Reading under their manager, former Blackpool star Harry Johnston, coaching in the mornings when he wasn't wanted by Yiewsley and also as a physical training instructor at Carmel College, the Jewish public school at Wallingford in Berkshire.

The call to go into the Football League came in January of 1963. Ipswich Town were the current First Division champions but their manager Alf Ramsey was about to take over as England boss with World Cup glory just three short years away.

Sixty people applied for the plum job but it eventually boiled down to just two — Milburn and Reg Flewin, the 43-year-old former centre-half of Portsmouth who was managing Stockport County. Jackie's interview with five directors lasted an hour then he and Laura went off to the pictures to await the board's decision.

'We were overwhelmed by the personality of the man,' explained Ipswich chairman John Cobbold afterwards.

Milburn, who refused the security of a contract, was to officially take over on April 29 when Ramsey was going to the Football Association but for the preceding weeks he was to work closely with his former England team-mate at Portman Road.

It was a top job, of course it was, working for the current champions with a board renowned for sticking by their manager and for a chairman with a reputation for not interfering or inflicting extra pressure. But really Milburn was walking into a minefield he didn't foresee, a club crumbling after the heady success of the previous season. Champagne was to be replaced with flat beer.

After the nightmare was over and things could be put into perspective Jackie told me: 'Ipswich were a First Division club with a Fourth Division team. We had no youth side and not a scout on the books. Alf lived in the town and visited the ground regularly, which didn't really help.

'The first season I somehow managed to keep Ipswich afloat but the second year I couldn't prevent them going down to the Second. Starting literally from rock bottom I wheeled and dealed and ended up flogging centre-forward Ray Crawford to Wolves so that I could buy Gerry Baker, Joe Broadfoot, Frank Brogan and Danny Hegan for peanuts. I still reckon they were good purchases at the price but time was always against us.

'My old mate Joe Harvey had taken over at Newcastle a year beforehand. United were heavily in debt and sinking fast towards the lower reaches of the Second Division. We were never off the phone to each other. Mentally, Joe was probably tougher than me. He was a man of iron will, a real Sergeant Major who made people jump. He battled his way through his crisis to achieve great things but for me it was all too much.'

The relegation season — 1963-64 — produced some results which Milburn, bred on success at Newcastle, found impossible to take. Ipswich lost 7-2 at home to Manchester United, 6-0 at Bolton, 6-0 at Liverpool, 9-1 at Stoke and 6-3 at Spurs. But the biggest humiliation of all came on Boxing Day. Ipswich went to Fulham and lost by a staggering 10-1 with Johnny Haynes pulling the strings, centre-forward Leggat scoring four and outside-left Howfield three. Afterwards Jack, his pride brutally hurt, had words with chairman Cobbold and a couple of players whom he thought were taking defeat too easily.

Sure, two days later there was some revenge with a 4-2 home win over Fulham in the return and there were moments of fleeting pleasure with victories over Burnley (3-1), West Ham (3-2), Birmingham (3-2), Nottingham Forest (4-3), Aston Villa (4-3) and Blackpool (4-3) but overall it was a period of total frustration.

'I was affected dreadfully. After yet another defeat I would sit in a darkened room, brooding for hours. For the one and only time in my life Jackie Milburn, a virtual non-drinker, turned to the bottle for solace. Without realising what I was doing I started drinking gin like it was going out of fashion. The side of my face even began to swell to grotesque shapes through worry after matches. It was all too much.'

Jackie offered to resign in the March following the 9-1 defeat at Stoke but Cobbold insisted: 'The last thing I want to see is Milburn go. Everyone likes him and I would not accept his resignation if he put it in writing.'

Four games into the new 1964-65 season in the Second Division, with only one point to show, Jackie couldn't stand it any longer.

'The response was immediate and, to a certain extent, reassuring given my depressed state. No fewer than nine players threatened to walk out if I were allowed to leave, which at least showed I had built up a sense of loyalty and communication. Billy Baxter and Gerry Baker led the revolt thinking I'd been sacked but it wasn't the case.

'Alf Ramsey had warned me that I needed new players but the money was limited. In 18 months I clocked up nearly 40,000 miles by car in my search for signings to say nothing of all the train and air journeys.

'I hadn't a chance really but what was nice was that when Bill McGarry eventually got them promotion he thanked me publicly for laying a good foundation for the club and three Ipswich directors did the same in front of everyone when they came to Sunderland for a match.'

The bottom line was that Jackie Milburn was just too nice to be a manager at the very highest level. The streak of ruthlessness in dealing with players — nastiness if you like — was missing from his make-up. All great managers have it. Jackie hadn't.

'As a player you are in charge of yourself but as a manager 11 other people hold your job in their hands. It's a very different sort of pressure. It was not my sort.'

Ipswich Town, however, never forgot him. They knew he was a special man and on his death printed a glowing tribute in the club programme.

CHAPTER THIRTEEN

Back Home

With Linfield, Yiewsley and Ipswich behind him the wandering Jackie became wor's again. He headed for Tyneside, the place where he was most comfortable amongst his own folk. Milburn himself often said to me: 'I've been to exotic places and fed on the best. You name the best rooms in the best hotels and I've had them — first class on the *Queen Mary* and all those things. But the only time I'm really happy is when I come back over the Tyne Bridge and smell the pit heaps. I'm back in Northumberland, the greatest place in the world.'

As a sports journalist, which is the job he settled into and held until illness sadly overtook him months before his death, he could indulge his interest in football without all the pressures of management.

Jack was never going to be a crusading journalist. He was far too gentle; criticism came hard. But he was to become a distinguished presence in the Press boxes of Newcastle United, Sunderland and Middlesbrough and his influence at St. James's Park could never be overstated. In the boardroom they would repeatedly listen to their most famous ex-star when appointing new managers.

And there were many significant milestones still to come . . . a sentimental testimonial match at St. James's when more than 45,000 turned out to pay homage, the offer of a full-time job back with his old club, the honour of being made a Freeman of the City along with Cardinal Basil Hume and the shock of Eamonn Andrews, red book tucked under his arm, confronting him as the subject of a *This Is Your Life* telly programme.

Jack was now a dear friend and a helping hand. My boyhood hero who had become a Press colleague, someone who shared my love of, and at times frustration with, Newcastle United. The genuine glory days had gone with Milburn's departure for Ireland — they have never won a top domestic honour since, coming the closest with two final defeats in the F.A. Cup and League Cup in the seventies. Perhaps that, plus his natural niceness and genuine star quality, combined to make him a highly popular figure on Tyneside. He could never walk down the street, even 30 years after his last game for United, without being stopped by admiring fans merely wanting a chat.

That adulation manifested itself in his testimonial match on May 10, 1967, the eve of his 43rd birthday and 10 years after he last pulled on the famous black and white shirt. Benefit games can be ten a penny with the public only showing lukewarm interest even if the player is still on the club's books.

There's a sameness about the games with no competitive edge and it takes a great star to conjure up enough interest to raise the crowd above the ordinary. Yet Jackie Milburn, 10 years on, pulled in an unbelievable 45,404 which is way, way above the present-day capacity of St. James's Park.

In a special interview I did with Jackie after his greatest ever tribute he told me: 'When the idea was first dreamed up by the Press and United's Supporters Club I was flattered but I never expected it to come off. Even when the directors gave their permission for the use of St. James's Park I still didn't believe the whole thing would go through. Soon the disbelief turned into panic. While arrangements were going on for the game a thought suddenly struck me: what if nobody bothered to turn up? Memories are short and 10 years is a long time. Most of the young supporters had never seen me kick a ball. I was just a name in a dusty record book.

'I was frightened to death right up to a couple of days before the game. If it hadn't been for Bobby Mitchell I might have packed it in. Mitch kept insisting the gate would be near 50,000 and some of his conviction began to rub off on me. Eventually a couple of days before the match I was convinced when there was hardly a ticket left to be sold.'

The band plays as Wor Jackie runs out for his testimonial match at St. James's Park on May 10, 1967 when a crowd of 45,404 turned up.

It was typical of a modest Milburn that he should worry but the public and the professionals rallied round. Bobby Charlton, Jimmy Armfield, Pat Crerand, Nobby Stiles, George Eastham and even that master Hungarian Ferenc Puskas, a roly poly figure with a left foot like a magic wand, all played on a night of vintage memories.

'Looking back I think what made the night was the old timers match before the big game. This was a sentimental occasion for me and my old mates. I got together United's 1951 Cup team — the greatest team it had ever been my privilege to play with. We turned out for 15 minutes each way against a team of ex-internationals like Len Shackleton, George Hardwick, Ivor Broadis, Tom Finney and Bob Hardisty. The fact that only 15 people came into the ground between seven o'clock, when the old timers match began, and the start of the big game proved what the 1951 team meant to them.

'This was the first time the side had been together since shortly after Wembley and the crowd wanted to pay their respects.'

The testimonial, which grossed a then record £8,200 for Milburn, beating Mitch's by £2,000, has stood out in my memory for the performance of three players apart from Jackie — Len Shackleton, Puskas and Bobby Charlton. Shack rarely played after retiring; his pride wouldn't let him. He wanted the fans to remember him at his very best. But for Milburn, his old mate from Hazlerigg Colliery, he made an exception . . . and went into secret training to get into reasonable shape. And the Clown Prince of Soccer unveiled his full repertoire, bending the ball with the outside of his foot and then dropping onto one knee beckoning the ball back with his finger as it duly obliged, and then hitting a banana shot which saw a bemused Jack Fairbrother put out the joint of his finger against the post as he tried in vain to stop it.

Charlton ran like a gazelle through a shocked defence to score the best goal of the night and Puskas was . . . well, Puskas. A player at the very height of his profession.

Milburn obliged, as he had to, with four goals and admitted candidly: 'When I stood in the centre circle alone at the start of the match with 45,500 folk cheering themselves hoarse it was the most moving moment of my entire career. The lump in my throat grew and grew until it almost choked the life out of me.'

Jackie had always been renowned for the sheer power of his shooting and it stayed with him even into retirement. I remember the Russians being amazed when he started peppering in shots during a Press kickaround at their Durham camp, while they were here for the 1966 World Cup finals and Jack, in suede shoes no less, was actually clocked faster than Leeds and Scotland hot shot Peter Lorimer during a session for an F.A. coaching manual.

When Milburn once remarked to Stanley Matthews that he would have loved to have had the dribbling ability of the great master Stan replied: 'Aye, and I would give anything to pack a shot like you!'

Talking of that Press kickaround we could have produced quite a team when we were together during United's Fairs Cup years with Wor Jackie, Albert Stubbins, Ivor Broadis and Len Shackleton all part of our corps. We often laughingly suggested we had more England internationals in the Press box than United had on the field!

His old Cup final skipper Joe Harvey was still manager of United when Milburn returned to the North East, of course, and the pair of them along with Shack used to play golf regularly together. Harvey, an underestimated manager in many ways, was

The author John Gibson with Wor Jackie at St. James's Park in 1978.

to win the Second Division Championship in 1965 and the European Fairs Cup in 1969 as well as take Newcastle to the 1974 F.A. Cup final.

'Joe had two sides to him, the tongue lasher and the lifter of sunken spirits. Such qualities are called man management. It stemmed from our playing days together.

'His first match after signing for us was against Blackpool at home. Within seconds of the start I pushed a ball back to him. It was a mile off the mark and went out of play. I was working at the pits at the time and thought no one could teach a miner how to swear. But never in my life had I heard such a torrent of abuse. All the lads heard it too, and got the message. Army man Joe was in charge.

'Players like Mitch, Tommy Walker and myself used to get a bit lax at times and we needed a touch of the verbals. On the other hand the likes of Charlie Crowe, Bobby Cowell and Ernie Taylor sometimes needed a boost and Joe psyched them up. I remember, for instance, little Ernie having a bad 'un one day. When Taylor had passed a decent ball Harvey stopped in mid stride, placed his hands on his hips and exclaimed: 'Ernie, there's not another man in this bloody game who could pass the ball like that.' You could see Taylor's chest puffing out and he was smartly back in the groove.

'As a manager Joe did the same. He'd put his arm round Terry Hibbitt, call him "my little general" and supply him with an endless stream of fags. And Malcolm Macdonald loved him like a father.

'What Joe did was combine those qualities with that special ingredient so vital to a boss: the ability to spot and sign real talent.'

In his years in the Press box Milburn always admired the artists, the men of skill or strikers of excitement. From the Harvey era he loved the vision of Hibbitt and Tony Green, the explosive power of SuperMac and the natural goalscoring knack of Pop Robson. The period of Gordon Lee and Richard Dinnis which followed was perhaps the least stimulating in terms of individual skill but Tommy Craig, though bought by Harvey, emerged to skipper the 1976 League Cup final side with his perceptive prompting on the left side of midfield which captured the heart of Milburn. And later he drooled over Chris Waddle and Paul Gascoigne, who as a chubby kid he called 'the greatest talent I've seen at St. James's in 30 years' long before he became a £2m player and won his first England cap.

Funnily enough, it was Jackie's brother-in-law Les Common, who was a scout for Newcastle, who first discovered the rare talent of Waddle long before he actually joined United. Les's involvement isn't widely known but he told me: 'I took Chris in for training when he was 12 but nothing happened and he finally drifted off to Coventry. That didn't work out because he was homesick and, though the big clubs weren't showing too much interest, I could see something in the lad. By now he was playing for my old club Tow Law and once, when manager Bill McGarry was at Jackie's house, I brought up the subject of Waddle once again. Sunderland had rejected him after a trial but this time United signed him though without too much enthusiasm.'

Eamonn Andrews surprises Jackie Milburn on *This Is Your Life* in 1981.

Waddle, like Gascoigne, went on to play for Spurs and England before he became the costliest player in British history with his staggering £4.25m transfer to French champions Marseille in the summer of 1989.

Milburn's legend and his personality inspired those who followed him in the cherished black and white of United. Pop Robson, for example, recalls his father, a lifelong Newcastle fan with Wor Jackie as his special hero, telling him as a kid: 'Play like him, son, and you'll reach the ultimate in football.'

Two men destined to take over Milburn's old No. 9 shirt, Wyn Davies and Malcolm Macdonald, harbour their own special memories.

'I first saw Jackie play on TV. It was the 1955 F.A. Cup final and I was 13 years old,' said Wyn the Leap whose aerial power confused and often destroyed the Continentals in United's European days. 'He was a brilliant player in a brilliant team and I never dreamt that one day I would follow in his footsteps. I got to know him when I came to Newcastle and quickly realised he was a man of warmth and integrity.'

SuperMac, years on, was prepared to learn from a past master in precisely the same way as Milburn learned from Gallacher as a player.

'Jackie had done it all in his time but was as desperate as the terrace fan for somebody to come and do it all again. He gave much advice over the years but I shall never forget the first. "You have 90 minutes to win the game. You are the match winner. Always ensure you have enough in you in the last minute to clinch victory."

'I've argued until I was blue in the face with coaches over this very point. Jackie taught me coaches coach but goalscorers win games and there was no one better than he at scoring and winning, and advising how to do it.'

Wor Jackie was the man behind the appointment of his old England team-mate Bill McGarry as boss in 1977.

'At the time United needed a troubleshooter to clear up the mess. They were in the middle of a players' revolt after the period of Gordon Lee and Richard Dinnis and there was no bigger troubleshooter in football than Bill McGarry. He revelled in his hard man tag, boasting that he was the most hated man in football but didn't give a damn as long as he was allowed to get on with the job.

'In the short term he was a success at Newcastle. He cleaned out the troublemakers, taught the players to keep quiet until they learned some responsibility for what they said, and put a little respect and dignity back in the club. Having put the house in order, however, he couldn't create a team of quality. He overstayed his time. Where he failed badly was in his transfer dealings. He bought badly far too often.'

McGarry, who came to the North East on his own without his family, almost lived at Jackie's house and it was Bill, realising the great potential in having a man of Milburn's dignity on the staff, who offered his pal a full-time job at the park. Jackie Milburn WAS Newcastle United in the same way as Matt Busby or Bobby Charlton were undisputedly part of Manchester United. They all had the same standing in football . . . good, decent men with a burning passion for their club and a perfect image. But whereas Busby and Charlton were later co-opted to the Old Trafford board Newcastle had never fully utilised the power of Milburn.

So it came about early in 1978 that Jack was offered the post of full-time youth development officer. It was the ideal job for Milburn, who would help recruit the kids who were to become tomorrow's stars. His ability to talk honestly and openly, with total conviction, to their fathers who probably saw Wor Jackie as a hero made him an inspired choice. But Jack's love of the quiet life saw him sadly and reluctantly turn down his old club. A few days later as we walked round a deserted St. James's Park he tried to explain to me why he had come to such a decision.

'Unquestionably it was the most agonising time of my life. There was so much pulling at my heartstrings. I could visualise the crowd roaring. A full house. There was Brennan, Taylor and Mitch. And I was scoring a goal. It was marvellous. A warm, warm glow.

'I never really left Newcastle United. Only my body walked out all those years ago. My heart stayed where it had always been. Going back seemed the most natural thing in the world, especially to work for my old mate Bill McGarry.

'I said yes to Bill and told the newspaper I was working for about my decision. It was all done and dusted. But then, as I drove away from St. James's, Bill told the Press I was coming back. A voice came over the car radio announcing that Jackie Milburn had rejoined United and for some reason I immediately felt uneasy.

'By the time I drove into our street I could see a TV camera crew and a posse of Press men on my doorstep. I panicked and, without realising it, instantly changed my mind about the job. I mumbled something about not having fully committed myself, about still having a few things to think over, and made it into the livingroom. I realised that, at the age of almost 54, I was heaping a load of pressure on my shoulders again. The sort of pressure I had never experienced since I quit as Ipswich Town's manager 12 years beforehand. I thought of the change in lifestyle and I shuddered. Literally.

'It's not that I doubted my ability to do the job. I knew I had that. No, it was going back into the public eye. To be truthful, I'd always been shy; found it hard to wear fame and bask in it. Even as a player I got embarrassed when lots of folk descended on me for my autograph. I was flattered — but I was scarlet. I don't bother with nightclubs or social clubs. They aren't my scene. I like the quiet life, playing a bit of golf and going caravanning with the missus. That's lovely. The smell of bacon and eggs in the morning and fresh air of the countryside. No ulcers there.'

The next night Milburn attended United's Cup replay with Peterborough. He vacated his usual seat in the Press box to watch from the back of the old stand and witness the game as he would see it from the Gallowgate payroll.

'My pulse was going 10 times faster than it ever had. I was watching the players through different eyes. It was a new game — I sweated non stop in the first-half when no goals came, felt drained and relieved in the second when we were home and dry. A few hours later I told Bill McGarry I couldn't do it. I was tempted and felt privileged to be asked but, no, it wasn't on. Luckily he understood.'

Milburn's contribution to Newcastle United was already unquestioned, of course, and just two years later — in July of 1980 — he was made a Freeman of the City of Newcastle at a colourful ceremony in the Civic Centre to mark the city's 900th anniversary. Also amongst nine new freemen was Cardinal Basil Hume, the Newcastle-born Roman Catholic Archbishop of Westminster and a great Jackie Milburn fan.

The last individual to have been so honoured was American President Jimmy Carter three years earlier and Jack's first reaction was: 'What's a pit lad doing in company like that?'

Cardinal Hume, who actually asked Milburn for his autograph, explained: 'He was not only a great footballer but a real gentleman and a person who instinctively won respect. There was a quality of goodness about him which inspired others. His goals at Wembley in the 50's remain etched in my mind.'

When Jackie fell ill only months before his death Cardinal Hume twice wrote beautifully warm letters to Laura giving them both comfort and hope at a period of intense family worry. I've seen the letters which Laura proudly keeps, along with the count-

Grandad Jackie with Katy and Laura, Betty's daughters.

less others from ordinary fans, tucked away in the drawer at her home in Ashington.

It was shortly after being made a Freeman of the City that Jack and I got together to write a book on United which led, indirectly, to his appearance on *This Is Your Life* towards the end of 1981. When the book came out it appeared on the desk of Brian Klein, a researcher for the programme at Thames Television. His job was to unearth suitable subjects for *This Is Your Life* and, with Jackie thrust back into the limelight through the publication of a new book, he looked an ideal candidate.

As co-writer of the book I received a phone call from Klein at the *Evening Chronicle* offices one afternoon. Jackie Milburn was under consideration for the show and would I co-operate? What followed was three months of meticulous work in total secrecy as the show was put together.

I had two key roles to play: it was to be my job to approach Laura for her permission and then to keep Jackie busy on the actual day of the programme so that he didn't become aware of what was going on. Both came at the most vulnerable time in the progression of a show which relies totally on the element of surprise. If Laura had said no there would have been no show and if Jackie had at any stage found out about it — even as late as the very day of recording — the plug would have been pulled.

Luckily Laura gave her agreement — albeit a little reluctantly knowing Jack's obsession with privacy — and I managed to keep the man himself busy on The Day. The one other problem was getting him to the studios. The *This Is Your Life* team knew they could never get Jack to London so it was agreed to bring the cameras out to Tyne Tees Television and a spoof programme entitled 'A Chance to Score' was set up. Milburn — and the audience for that matter — believed he was to be interviewed about our new book and even then Jackie would have preferred it had I looked after it alone. But with a little gentle persuasion — you know, do it for me knowing full well that Jack would never let a friend down — we got the show on the road.

United's current boss Arthur Cox helped me keep Milburn busy on the day and when Jack walked through the audience to warm applause the red curtains suddenly swished back and there was Eamonn Andrews, beaming that smile which says 'gotcha!' Jack almost collapsed with shock.

But the next half hour was pure nostalgia. Apart from his family and personal friends a host of celebrities walked on . . . Bobby and Jack Charlton, his old England captain Billy Wright, Tom Finney, Raich Carter and goalkeeper Bert Trautmann, who had conceded that Jackie goal after only 45 seconds of the 1955 F.A. Cup final. To top it all Jackie's aunt Bella was flown across from New York, the first time the couple had met in 31 years.

'Talk about getting a surprise. I was flabbergasted,' Jackie told me at the reception afterwards. 'How on earth did you keep it a secret? I wouldn't have gone, you know, if I'd had an inkling. But I'm glad I did. It was a special occasion.'

Cox, who produced delightful days in the Second Division with Kevin Keegan, Chris Waddle and Peter Beardsley, was actually followed at St. James's for one short season by big Jack Charlton in 1984-85.

It meant one of the Milburn Clan back at Newcastle, of course, and that pleased Jackie who always felt it was an advantage if the manager had a definite feel for the area.

Jack Charlton was Jackie Milburn's half cousin . . . Cissie Charlton's father Tanner Milburn and Jackie's dad Alec were brothers. Cissie, whose real name is Elizabeth, had married Bob Charlton, a miner at Linton Colliery whose sporting bent was boxing not football. The day Bob took on the fairground pug at Paddy's Market he got paid a pound for his troubles. With it he bought Cissie a wedding ring for 17s 6d and a kerb for the fireplace for 2s 6d. They moved into Laburnum Terrace, a typical row of pit houses, and eventually had four sons, Jackie, Bobby, Tommy and Gordon.

It was almost inevitable with Cis's background that her sons should turn to football. As a child her toys were not dolls but football boots, footballs and marbles. During the summer she would train on Newbiggin beach with her famous brothers Jack, George, Jim and Stan Milburn and 'curse a thousand times over that I was born a lass.' Everyone called her Cis, short for sister, probably because Elizabeth was hardly the sort of name to shout on a football pitch, however makeshift.

Jackie and Bobby were never alike in any way. Jackie was the mixer, bubbling over with life and fun like his mother. Bobby was shy to the point where people misguidedly called him a big head.

'As kids Jackie was always the rascal going bird nesting and shooting at the lasses with a gun out of the bedroom window,' Cissie told me. 'Bobby never got into any mischief. He used to be nicknamed Little Lord Fauntleroy!'

Bobby, two and a half years younger, was the natural footballer; a player of grace and style who had Football League clubs goggle eyed at his ability. Jackie was a gangling 6ft 2in tall with the build of a toothpick when he left school.

'Although he will never admit it I know that Len Shackleton was Bobby's hero,' said Cissie. 'Shack had a habit of pulling his shirt sleeves over his hands and taking his shinguards out during a game. Subconsciously Bobby began doing the same. He would dearly have liked to have signed for Sunderland but when they sent a scout along to watch him play for East Northumberland Boys in 1953 he ignored Bobby and made a beeline for the goalkeeper Ronnie Routledge.

'Bobby was so hurt he said he'd sign for any club that came

along after that. I was still consoling him on the touchline when Manchester United's scout Joe Armstrong came over.'

While Bobby became a legend at Old Trafford Jackie made his name with Leeds United, the only club to show an interest in him according to Cissie.

When I asked Cissie why neither joined Newcastle United when her cousin, Jackie Milburn, was the hero she replied: 'They were never interested in Jack and only sent Ted Hughes, who was in charge of the juniors, after Bobby had agreed to go to Old Trafford.'

Jack loved 'the toon', however, and now at long last he had joined them as manager. He was a brilliant coach who had been voted Manager of the Year when helping Middlesbrough win the Second Division championship by the proverbial mile but he was a man who wouldn't allow any player to buck his authority, often creating the wrong impression, and his greatest weakness was his buying in the transfer market.

United had just won promotion to the First Division under Cox, who bought flair, and while Jack's coaching ability meant the club were never in any danger in their first season back in the top flight he didn't buy the sort of personality players who had marked the Harvey and Cox eras.

He'd often said: 'If the fans don't want me I'll be off like a shot' and, sure enough, he upped and quit on the spot when supporters began heckling at a pre-season friendly. It was typical of the impetuous Charlton — I firmly believe he lived to regret such a rash decision — but, once made, he was always going to stand by it. Wor Jackie was saddened to see him go, which is natural considering a relation was leaving the club he loved above all others.

'He shouldn't have resigned. He could have made it work in the end. But then Jack was always a bit hot headed.'

By the summer of 1988 Milburn was not at all well. Always a smoker, he was suffering from chest pains to such an extent that his treasured golfing days with Laura were abandoned and he retired from his job with the *News of the World* newspaper. His cheerful face and his expertise were to be sadly missed from the Press boxes of the North East.

In the next few months apprehension grew. Jackie withdrew into the bosom of his family, retaining his dignity as his illness progressed. Those of us who knew him well could understand. He didn't want us to see him fighting bravely for life. It was too painful, too personal. For three long months Laura nursed him with all the care and the love in the world. The family doctor called her effort 'magnificent'. Jackie junior and Betty lent a hand but everyone else — even relatives — respected his wish for privacy.

On October 9, 1988 Wor Jackie died of lung cancer without ever once giving up the battle. We had known what lay ahead but the shock and feeling of utter loss was still overwhelming. A great man had passed away at the early age of 64.

Tyneside, indeed the whole of the North East, was stunned. He had always been one of the people, in some ways their leader if you like, and now he was gone. The mourning which took place had never been surpassed even by the most distinguished of political leaders in the area.

More than 30,000 lined the streets from his terraced home in Ashington to St. Nicholas's Cathedral in the centre of Newcastle on the day of his funeral. Men, women and children — many with tears in their eyes and wearing black and white scraves — stood silently as his funeral cortege, led by two police motorcyclists, passed by.

At the cathedral there was another huge turn-out. All 900 seats were taken up, some of the public arriving two hours early, and there was standing room for a couple of hundred more at the back. Outside another 2,000 gathered.

Ashington vicar, the Rev. Philip Bennison, told the congregation: 'Jack had such an infinite patience with people. There was a young girl in Ashington, a Brownie, who asked Jackie if he would help her with a project. He spent hours with her, showing her his medals, trophies, and explaining all about the game. She has not forgotten that kindness and is here today.

'People throughout the region who knew Jack Milburn always wondered at his capacity to see the good in people, not the bad. Witness the people here today: they have come from far and wide, not only because Jack was a famous footballer but because, I feel, he was a genuine and loving man.

'For the family, football and fame were a small part of their lives. In the last few weeks when Jack was dying they saw it as a time of peace. He was determined that the family should go on — that man of strength and elegance was so weak that he would come down stairs on his bottom to join his loved ones. All the family watched his final peace.

'Perhaps that was best expressed by his six-year-old granddaughter Laura who had a special relationship with her grandad. She came to me on the evening I called and said: "You know Jesus and talk to him, don't you? Well, I bought this out of my own money so will you give it to Jesus and ask him to pass it on to grandad?"

'I have in my hand her gift — a fish shaped bottle of bubble bath as Jackie had told her that when there was thunder about it was the angels playing football. She naturally presumed he would be playing in heaven's first division and thought it might come in handy after the match.'

Following the service the cortege once again significantly snaked its way past St. James's Park, the home of so many of Wor Jackie's triumphs, on its way to the city's West Road crematorium.

A proud region had mourned its favourite son and on both national TV channels that night the pictures were beamed round the land.

Jack Charlton reflected: 'Jackie didn't like the big crowds or occasions but I think he would have appreciated his send off. The atmosphere was one of such love and respect for a fine footballer that tears were mixed with a feeling of wanting to applaud one last time.'

Sadly for me Jackie had died while I was on a short holiday in Portugal and Laura, knowing my personal feelings and my wish to say goodbye, kindly asked me to say a few words at a memorial service held at the Church of the Holy Sepulchre in Ashington a little while later. Once again the place was packed to the rafters.

My speech wasn't written or even thought out. It came from where it matters: the heart. Jackie Milburn had always played that way and it was the only way to pay tribute to him.

CHAPTER FOURTEEN

Remembering . . .

Jackie Milburn was so loved that his death brought a spate of tributes to a distinguished man. Newcastle United, who were always his first love, named their newly-built main stand The Milburn Stand and his ashes were scattered at his beloved Gallowgate end where his greatest fans always congregated and where he scored so many spectacular winners.

A musical, *Wor Jackie*, toured the North East to unbridled acclaim, a national TV company moved into Ashington to research an hour-long documentary on him, and the *Evening Chronicle* launched a public appeal to raise cash for a bronze statue of him to be unveiled in the centre of town — an unheard of tribute to a footballer with all other monuments being erected long ago in honour of political figures.

The fuss and the clamour were enormous and, I'm sure, would have amused and bewildered a man who always insisted: 'All I ever did was kick a football aroond!'

That was over-simplification, of course. What Milburn actually did was unite an area in admiration for an artist of genius. He also lived among them and was always available to them, never developing the pretentious lifestyle of today's footballers.

Albert Stubbins, an early Milburn hero who became a team-mate, saw the attraction in obvious terms: 'He was the ideal footballer for the Newcastle fans, a demanding and knowledgeable crowd who positively venerate the centre-forward. He was exciting and appealing. He wasn't conceited. He was a gentleman,

The huge crowds outside the cathedral in Newcastle for Jackie's funeral in October, 1988.

a genuinely unassuming man, not hypocritical about his modesty. He played in three winning Cup finals in which he was the star performer, in a phase of Newcastle's history which will never be repeated. He symbolised it all. He was completely a Geordie. He loved his native Ashington. And he never changed his accent.'

A musical on a footballer may have raised a few eyebrows. Transferring a sport which needs a high degree of natural skill to the boards, or to the screen, has never proved to be easy — but then making the main characters sing into the bargain seemed ambitious in the extreme.

But *Wor Jackie* worked. Football's anthems, whether they be the Blaydon Races or You'll Never Walk Alone, are strong, powerful songs which somehow blend with the bold artistry of the game. And so did both the music and lyrics in *Wor Jackie*:

> This is the story of Jack and the glory
> that he brought to the small pit town.
> He used his feet to blast away the shackles,
> and the walls came a-tumbling down . . .

Frank Gibbon, whose band once toured with the likes of Captain Beefheart and Slade, wrote the music with Rick Taylor and says: 'I played football for the regional county team and Jackie Milburn in those days was literally The Man. I took my bugle and played it at the Gallowgate end. The beauty about those days was that they didn't smear themselves in liniment and they didn't earn a fortune. The money didn't matter — it was doing it that was important.'

The writers, Mike Kirkup and Keith Armstrong, both have strong roots in the region and they approached Jackie before his death to talk about the musical which, in fact, sadly didn't open until after he died. Jackie gave his blessing, albeit a little warily, but the finished product was such that it won a £12,000 prize in a London Weekend Television competition.

Colin MacLachlan, who played Wor Jackie in later life, came into the *Evening Chronicle* offices to spend hours talking to me about the man and browsing through our files on him.

'It's amazing,' Colin told me. 'Everyone talks of him with such love, not just affection. No one has a bad word to say about Jackie Milburn.'

Index